BRIGHT NOTES

THE LEFT HAND OF DARKNESS BY URSULA LE GUIN

Intelligent Education

Nashville, Tennessee

BRIGHT NOTES: The Left Hand of Darkness
www.BrightNotes.com

ISBN: 978-1-645425-20-5 (Paperback)
ISBN: 978-1-645425-21-2 (eBook)

Originally published by Monarch Press.
Rebecca Rass, 1990
2019 Edition published by Influence Publishers.

Interior design by Lapiz Digital Services. Cover Design by Thinkpen Designs.

Printed in the United States of America.

Library of Congress Cataloging-in-Publication Data forthcoming.
Names: Intelligent Education
Title: BRIGHT NOTES: The Left Hand of Darkness
Subject: STU004000 STUDY AIDS / Book Notes

CONTENTS

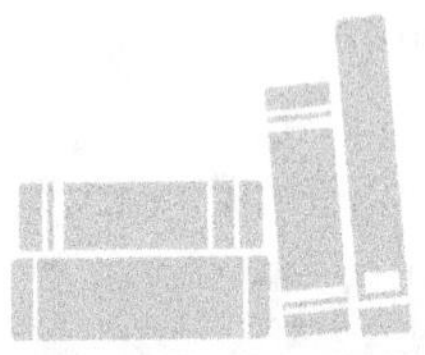

INTRODUCTION TO URSULA LE GUIN

THE LEFT HAND OF DARKNESS: ITS PLACE IN THE HISTORY OF SCIENCE FICTION

Male dominance

The first science fiction novel, it is largely agreed, was written by a woman, Mary Shelley, the daughter of the feminist Mary Wollstonecraft and the wife of the English romantic poet Shelley. She wrote *Frankenstein* in 1818 when she was only nineteen. However, the field has since been dominated by male writers who have made the domain of science fiction almost exclusively male. Indeed, in his book *Billion Year Spree - The True History of Science Fiction*, Brian Aldiss describes the **genre** as an "all-male escapist power fantasy" and calls its writers "Philistine-male-chauvinist pigs" who work in the "Ghetto of Retarded Boyhood."

Immature heroes

The heroes that these male writers created were generally immature men seeking to remain forever young and powerful, playing with imaginative and powerful toys, hoping to escape from girls or women, mothers or wives, as well as to avoid the responsibilities of a demanding reality, enclosing themselves in their exclusive men's club.

Female heroine followers

Needless to say, all these heroes were virile males served by their followers, the female characters. With all their invention and often daring imagination, these writers failed to explore alternative roles for women in a future society. Jules Verne and H.G. Wells, the lions in the **genre**, had hardly any place for women in their fantasies. Other writers who did employ female characters pictured the relationships between the heroes and their women largely along the same lines as did the existing society: women as assistants to men, women in the role of entertaining dolls. A classic example is the story "Helen O'Loy" by Lester del Rey (1938) which features a man who builds a robot programmed to be a perfect wife. These writers, naturally, aimed their stories mainly at male readers, mostly young boys who often stopped reading science fiction novels once they grew up.

No women writers

In her fine introduction to *Women of Wonder*, Pamela Sargent, herself a prolific science-fiction writer, calls traditional science fiction "an escapist literature for men and boys." She claims that women have traditionally been discouraged from entering scientific and technological fields, based on two assumptions: first, that women lack the aptitude, and second, that they are essentially intuitive rather than rational, and are "hostile to any kind of intellectual exploration."

Few women dared to invade the field and even when they did, they imitated their male colleagues. Catherine Moore, for example, wrote from the male point of view, "a necessity," Pamela Sargent explains, "for anyone who wished to publish in the pulp magazines which had dominated American SF since the 1920s."

Change

A change began to take place after World War II, when some women science-fiction writers joined the field. However, they too, like their male colleagues, usually presented housewife heroines, passive, naive, ignorant child-raisers, who solve problems not through their intelligence and daring but through ineptitude or accident.

Only in the 1960s, a decade that gave birth to much questioning of **conventions** as well as to many social revolutions (including feminism), women science-fiction writers began to question the very nature of science fiction, and as a result, took it in a completely new direction: software replaced hardware, human relationships replaced technology, social science took the place of the physical sciences. Substance and emotional content introduced depth and meaning into what had often been flat, boy scouts' literature.

Women writers

In 1973 Brian Aldiss said that much of the best writing in science fiction of that time was done by women who brought the **genre** closer to mainstream fiction. Although there was still much

"Sword-and-Sorcery" writing in the market, the best of science fiction is more reality-oriented, reflected in better and more careful writing, better characterization, and more diversity of subjects.

Although much of today's science-fiction writing is still male-oriented power fantasies, serious writers such as Ursula Le Guin or Joanna Russ have turned the best of science fiction into writing worthy of serious consideration and literary criticism. Pamela Sargent, in her introduction to *Women of Wonder*, presents an intriguing quote by Harlan Ellison: "... women are writing many of the things male SF writers thought could never be written, they are opening up whole new areas to us ..."

Rise in popularity

Darko Suvin, a Canadian critic, surveying contemporary science fiction, maintains that science fiction has risen in popularity in the leading industrial nations, especially among college graduates and the general population interested in alternative ways of thinking. This increase is attributed to the fact that from the early 1970s on, an increasing number of courses in science-fiction literature have been offered in universities worldwide.

Background of The Left Hand of Darkness

In the light of this history, Ursula Le Guin's *Left Hand of Darkness*, first published in 1969, presents a real change. Human relationships take center stage; everything else is subordinate to the development of a profound and meaningful relationship between two human beings. The great achievement of *The Left Hand of Darkness* is the creation not of a new technology or of science-fiction gadgets but rather of a new society of truly equal human beings. It is her depth of thought, emotional involvement, strong moral values, and philosophical thinking that place Le Guin among the very top contemporary science-fiction writers.

Feminist book

In her article "Is Gender Necessary?" Le Guin herself openly discusses what inspired her to write *The Left Hand of Darkness.* It was, she writes, in the mid-1960s when the women's movement began to awaken after half a century of stagnation. Although as a writer she had never been treated unfairly or patronizingly on account of her sex, Le Guin was bothered by the question that besieged many women then and even now: What is a woman? This question had motivated the French philosopher and writer, Simone de Beauvoir, to write what has been considered the bible of the women's movement, *The Second Sex* (France 1949, United States 1953), the exploration of women's situation throughout the ages. This question also inspired the American feminist Betty Friedan to write *The Feminine Mystique* (1963).

In "Is Gender Necessary?", written in 1976, seven years after the publication of *The Left Hand of Darkness*, Le Guin, suprisingly, rejected the notion that hers was a "feminist" book. Although she considered herself a feminist (holding that every thinking woman is a feminist), she emphasized that "the real subject of the book is not feminism or sex or gender ... it is a book about betrayal and fidelity." However, in 1987, eleven years later, Le Guin revised her essay, or rather added comments that attest to her own growth as a conscious feminist. In "Is Gender Necessary? Redux", she admits to having been defensive and resentful that critics had concentrated on the gender problems "as if it were an essay, not a novel." In her revision she writes that "there are other aspects of the novel" inextricably involved with its gender aspects.

In *The Left Hand of Darkness* Le Guin has aspired to reach beyond the question of "What is a woman?" to broader and deeper questions of "What is sexuality?" and "What is the meaning of gender?" Besides physiological differences, are there really any differences between men and women? Being a novelist, her explorations of these questions are the basis of *The Left Hand of Darkness.*

To be precise, the book does not offer ultimate answers, and readers will not find there the answer to the basic question of "What is a woman?" Actually, when the male Envoy from Earth is asked by his friend from the new planet to explain what a woman is, he embarrassedly hesitates, fails, and finally admits that he does not know what a woman is. But more important than the answers are the questions and the hypothesis that Le Guin offers, in her "thought-experiment," as she calls the novel in her intriguing introduction. The book serves as "the record of my consciousness, the process of my thinking" in the laboratory of the mind. It offers alternative modes of thinking not about the future but about ourselves in the present.

The result? "Messy," according to Le Guin, "dubious and uncertain." The same experiment done by someone else, she maintains, and even by herself several years later, "would probably give quite different results" (in her revision she replaces the word "probably" by "certainly").

However, Le Guin has been frequently criticized for making her Gethenians, although they are menwomen, too much like men. Feminists have accused her of not going far enough and for using male protagonists. In her recent essay, "The Fisherman's

Daughter" (1988), Le Guin admits that these critics were right, that until the mid-1970s "men were the central characters, the women were peripheral, secondary." And she adds that feminism has empowered her to criticize her society, herself, and feminism itself.

All that aside, however, in the *New Republic*, Derek de Solla Price emphasizes that he knows of no "single book [that is] likely to raise consciousness about sexism more thoroughly and convincingly than this one."

INTRODUCTION TO URSULA LE GUIN URSULA K. LE GUIN'S LIFE AND WORK: AN INTERVIEW

THE WRITER AND THE WOMAN

Ursula K. Le Guin draws a sharp line between herself as a person, woman, wife and mother and herself as a writer. An introvert, she jealously keeps her private life to herself, shielding her family and her private self from the limelight.

In her entire body of stories and novels nothing is autobiographical. Her friends and family members will not find themselves in her books as is so often the case with fiction writers. Although the integration of polarities emerges as a central **theme** in her writing, it seems that hers is a sharply divided world between the private and the professional.

Her answer to my request for a telephone interview came in the form of a short letter, with a don't-call-me-I'll-call-you provision, ardently defending her telephone number as others defend their valuables.

Is this one reason why she writes science fiction, for the distancing effect that creates the maximum remoteness between Le Guin the writer and Le Guin the woman? "Is science fiction the best way to guard her privacy? "I don't want to write autobiographies," she said once. "I want to distance myself from my books. That's one of the reasons I write science fiction. I write about aliens."

POLITICAL ACTIVIST

So I was truly surprised to hear a warm and melodious voice over the telephone. She apologized for not calling the day before as agreed. I was happy she had not called then because on the previous day I had joined other writers in a demonstration for freedom of speech concerning the Salman Rushdie affair. "Oh, that's what we did here!" she exclaimed. (Rushdie's novel *The Satanic Verses* had provoked Iran's Ayatollah Khomeini to order his assassination.)

Here was a glimpse of Le Guin the person, after all. It was typical of her, putting her writing aside and throwing herself into a social or political cause she believes in. In the 1960s she became involved in the peace demonstrations and campaigned for Eugene McCarthy and then George McGovern in their primaries. Her political activities in the peace movement led to a short novel, *The Eye of the Heron*, and to *The Word for World Is Forest*, and then to *The Left Hand of Darkness*, considered by many to be her best work.

NO-WAR SOCIETY

Her voice was pleasant and relaxed as we talked about the genesis of her book. "It all started when I began to imagine a society without war, a people that does not think in terms of war.

They have murders and forays but never wars. What kind of people would they be? I thought. Obviously, they'd be different from us. But in what way? That's how I came to the idea of an androgynous society. As one character says in the book, war is a displaced male-generalized activity, something that men do and women don't." War, as she defines it in her book, is "a vast Rape."

WHY SCIENCE FICTION?

Still, the question of why a talented and versatile writer like herself has chosen science fiction, a **genre** considered by the mainstream literary world as marginal, is still there. One reason, as said before, is her need to distance herself and her private life from her subjects. But as with all else in Ursula Le Guin, the reasons for her writing science fiction are complex and many.

A JOURNEY INWARD

At one time she explained that fantasy is the best medium to describe the journey inward to self-knowledge, because for her, the journey to other planets, to outer space, is a **metaphor** for the journey inward into the unconscious. This inner journey cannot be described in the language of rational everyday life, she said. Fantasy is the natural language for telling "the spiritual journey and the struggle of good and evil in the soul."

CHILDHOOD

Perhaps the first reason for her writing can be traced to her childhood, growing up with parents who both were writers, scholars, and excellent story tellers. Born in Berkeley, California, on October 21, 1929, Ursula K. Le Guin was the youngest child of Theodora and Alfred Kroeber. Her mother, after earning her master's degree in clinical psychology, married, and three years later, with two babies, was widowed. Later she married Alfred Kroeber, and had another son and her youngest and only daughter, Ursula. When her own children were having their children, Theodora, now in her fifties, began to write, making a name for herself with the biography of the sole survivor of an Indian tribe wiped out by North Americans, Ishi in Two Worlds (1961).

Ursula's father, Alfred Kroeber, was an anthropologist who spoke several languages and was renowned for his work on the California Indians. Even before she could read, Ursula would listen to her father tell Indian legends and myths.

THE MAKING OF A WRITER

This home was an excellent greenhouse for nurturing a writer, and Ursula, from an early age, enjoyed the best training in psychology, anthropology, sociology, and writing. "I had an emotionally and psychologically and intellectually very rich and very serene childhood," she told me. "I loved where we lived. I had a large, warm family. It was a place where a small girl could grow and flourish like a flower in the garden."

As a child Ursula read everything she could get her hands on: myths, legends, fairy tales. Once, when she was about twelve, she picked up a book in the family's large library, and while reading it, she was struck by the realization that people were still making up stories and myths! It was a decisive moment. She had discovered her native country and her inner lands.

BEGINNING TO WRITE

In fact, she had completed her first short story three years earlier, when she was only nine. It was about a man persecuted by elves. A year later she wrote her first science fiction story about time travel. She submitted it for publication but the story was rejected, and she did not try to publish her work again until the age of 19.

READING

Instead, she plunged into reading, and there is no better apprenticeship for a writer than reading, She read mostly fiction, poetry, and science fiction, some of it trash, "because we liked trash." In her teens she stopped reading science fiction and did not read it for fifteen years, because it was too much about "hardware and soldiers"; instead, she turned to the classics.

HIGHER EDUCATION

She graduated from Radcliffe College with a major in French in 1951 and earned her master's degree in French and Italian from Columbia University in 1952. A year later she began to study for her Ph.D. and won a Fulbright grant to study in France.

FAMILY LIFE

Crossing the Atlantic on the Queen Mary, she met her future husband, Charles Le Guin, a professor of French history. Their marriage in Paris signaled the end of her doctoral studies and the beginning of a long and happy family life which later included two daughters and a son. In 1959 Charles was assigned to teach history at Portland State University and the family has lived in Portland, Oregon, ever since.

REJECTED MANUSCRIPTS

Giving up her work on the doctorate allowed Le Guin more time to write. She kept writing and watching her drawers fill up with manuscripts and rejection slips. In ten years she had written, aside from poetry, five novels, some about a fantasy country in Central Europe named Orsinia, but none was accepted for publication. It became for her a matter of "publish or perish." Her fantasies did not fit any existing category, and if she wanted to publish she would have to find an acceptable form. She began to write science fiction.

PUBLICATION

Le Guin admits that her "first efforts to write science fiction were motivated by a pretty distinct wish to get published." Not having much hard-core scientific knowledge she wrote "fairy tales decked out in space suits." It paid: she got them published. She was 32 when she managed to sell her first story, "April in Paris," to *Fantastic* magazine (1962). Her first science fiction novel to be published was *Rocannon's World* (1966). This signaled the beginning of a brilliant career that has produced science fiction stories and novels, children's and young adults' books, essays and poetry. "I have cut across so many boundaries that the critics don't know what to do with me," she laughs over the phone. "I write in so many categories."

SUCCESS

Two more science fiction novels, *Planet of Exile* (1966) and *City of Illusion* (1967), followed almost immediately, but her real success came with the publication of *A Wizard of Earthsea* (1968) which won the prestigious Globe-Hornbook Award for Excellence. With the award came national recognition. Then, *The Left Hand of Darkness* (1969) won both the Hugo and Nebula Awards, and when her novel *The Dispossessed* (1974) appeared and also won the Hugo and Nebula, Le Guin became the first science fiction writer to have won both awards twice.

It would take too long to list all her books and stories and all the awards and prizes she has won. Just reaching her 60s, Le Guin no doubt will continue to add considerably to both lists.

MODEL FEMINIST

Many feminists have complained that Ursula Le Guin's characters are predominantly male, and even her Gethenians, the people on planet Winter, who are both men and women in one, appear to be basically male. However, her own life can serve as a model of the successful, modern, sophisticated, and liberated woman who has managed a brilliant career, successful marriage, and motherhood, without sacrificing any of them.

"When the kids were babies I wrote at night, from nine to eleven or as long as I could stay awake. Then, as they began school, I had the whole schoolday to work; I felt as if I grew wings. Now, I try to work in the morning, from about seven to two."

PARTNERSHIP

She could manage her writing because of the steady support of her husband. Theirs was a partnership with "mutual aid as its daily basis." They divided the work conventionally: she, the house, the kids, the cooking, the novels; he, the teaching, the bills, the car, the garden. When she needed help he gave it "without making it into a big favor"; when she wanted to complete a story, he would take the kids. "He never begrudged me the time I spent writing, or the blessing of my work." It is difficult for one person to do two full-time jobs but two people can do three full-time jobs, she said. "That's why I'm so strong on partnership. It can be a great thing."

No wonder that love, bonding, and intimate relationship take such a significant place in all her work! This is the one idea that overrides everything else in *The Left Hand of Darkness*. Moreover, in this book she carries the idea even further and maintains that true love between individuals must precede, and is the only basis for, national, international, or universal relations.

THE MALE WRITER

"Does your happy and fulfilled life refute the notion that a writer has to suffer in order to write?" I asked her. This made her burst out in peals of laughter. "I think that this notion seems to suit men wonderfully well. They love to smite their brow with their hand and say, 'Oh, how I suffer,' while some woman is actually doing all the work. I'm quite leery of this idea. I think writing is quite hard enough work without complaining about all the rest. I get impatient with Conrad or Flaubert who, while complaining, were actually being looked after very nicely. They were not really handling the complicated part of life that any woman has to handle if she has responsibilities for the household or of getting the meals. You know, as I watch women writers, I see them cope with it all along with their art, and we are talking here about real work, not psychological suffering."

THE PRICE OF LOVE

Le Guin seems to have been blessed with a happy family life as a child and as an adult. Yet in her novels and essays she refers again and again to pain and suffering as a necessary price for happiness. In *The Left Hand of Darkness*, the moment Ai gains profound love he also loses it. Where had her experience of sorrow come from? I wondered.

TRAGIC SENSE OF LIFE

There was silence at the other end of the line, and I wondered whether she was thinking the question over or looking for ways to avoid touching upon her private life. "I guess," she finally said, "one carries in oneself a tragic sense of life. If you believe, as I do, that the great tragedies, such as Sophocles' or Shakespeare's, were the truest things ever written, then you know that what is within our grasp is essentially tragic."

In *The Left Hand of Darkness* she wrote that the only certainty a person has is his mortality, the knowledge that he is going to die.

"Yes. No matter how lucky one can be, there is considerable suffering involved in being alive, in being human."

"There is a strong sense of inescapable tragedy in your book," I said.

"I agree. I realize that underneath everything I write there is this sense of the tragic. This is the way I'm made, how I see life. It doesn't mean I don't appreciate life. I see much of my writing, but mainly my poetry, as celebration and I like writing which is celebration."

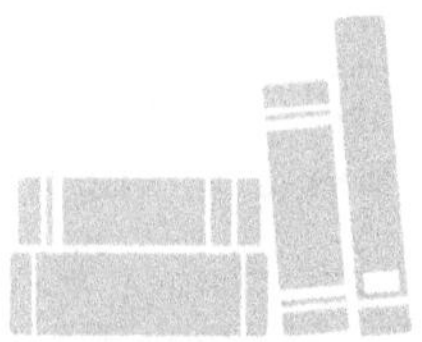

INTRODUCTION TO THE LEFT HAND OF DARKNESS

We resumed talking about the genesis of the book. "A book like that," she said, "doesn't have any single beginning. As I mentioned before, first I had the idea of creating a society without war. This led me to the androgynous society. Then I had the characters. And as the characters began to interact I began to see the plot. I saw two people dragging a sledge across the ice."

"My favorite part in the book," I commented.

"Mine, too, "she said enthusiastically. "I had to do a great deal of work before I began writing. I had to figure out how an androgynous society actually works. Also, I had to do a good deal of reading about living in a very cold climate."

WINTER

"I never quite understood," I admitted, "how the bitter cold climate on Winter, which features so prominently in the book, is connected with the idea of androgyny?"

"I have no idea," came her clear answer. "One of those underground connections, I guess. I can probably explain it less well than a critic. I don't think it is particularly linked to the sexual issue. The link in my mind is to loneliness, Ai's loneliness for being one of his kind on the planet, and to Estraven's, because he has isolated himself. This is a story of extremely lonely people coming together, and the cold accentuates, and reflects their loneliness. Before I began writing I read Winter in Finland, which was very helpful. I wanted to know what one does when it's 30 below zero for a month!"

PREPARATION FOR THE BOOK

"Also, I read what I could concerning the special sexuality of the people on the planet. I checked out human sexual physiology, but to tell you the truth, I didn't have the courage till after the book was printed, to take it to a doctor and ask: Is this plausible? It was our pediatrician. He read it and he gave it back to me, saying it's plausible but it's disgusting!" (She laughed merrily). "I thought it was charming. 'Yes, it did work,' he said, 'you did it pretty convincingly.'

"I also had to write the history of both countries on the planet Winter. It's not in the book, but it underlines it. How did the two countries get to where they are now? Why are they as they are?"

STRONGER FEMINIST

"In your article 'Is Gender Necessary?' you write that *The Left Hand of Darkness* is not about gender but about betrayal and fidelity - "

"Have you seen the revised article?" she interrupted excitedly. "This is very important for me. I have a new book that just came out, *Dancing at the Edge of the World*, and in that you'll find a revised version. Nothing has been changed in the text, but notes and comments have been added, where I disagree violently with some of the things I myself have said there. I have become a much stronger feminist and my thinking is considerably clearer since I wrote the book, which was itself part of my becoming a feminist."

Several essays in *Dancing at the Edge of the World* present strong and clear feminist statements. In "Woman / Wilderness" Le Guin criticizes civilization for leaving out the experience of women as women, an experience unshared with men. "The misogyny that shapes every aspect of our civilization," she wrote, excluded "the being of women." Another essay, "Prospects for Women in Writing" ends with a strong proclamation and a feminist commitment: "To keep women's words, women's works, alive and powerful - that's what I see as our job as writers and readers for the next fifteen years, and the next fifty."

A major flaw in *The Left Hand of Darkness*, as Le Guin herself came to admit and as many of her critics expressed, is as she says, "that the Gethenians seem like men, instead of men-women."

This flaw is mainly the result of her use of the masculine pronoun he. While Le Guin is very imaginative in her use of language-in inventing names and places and landscapes that do not exist-in this novel she has used a quite traditional grammatical structure which, in English, is strictly divided along masculine-feminine lines. Reluctant to invent a new pronoun to herald the new age of human beings, equal in life and in language (it would drive the reader mad, she claimed), she preferred to use the masculine pronoun, which, in many ways, negated the main idea in the book.

It is strange, even inexplicable, that even at times when she could have used the neuter "people" or "human being" or "person" or "child" or "youth," she stubbornly has used explicitly male words such as "man" and "son." Even the woman investigator in *The Left Hand of Darkness* admits that "the very use of the pronoun in my thoughts leads me continually to forget that the Karhider I am with is not a man, but a manwoman." And if the woman reporter who meets the Karhiders face to face prefers to call them "he" and not "she," one may conclude that as Le Guin presents them, they do resemble men. This greatly diminishes the overall impact of the original idea of a sexless society.

PARENTHOOD

It is interesting to note that the Gethenians, who can be both mother and father, feel closer to the children "of their flesh," those to whom they actually gave birth. Estraven writes to his son of the flesh but does not mention the other two children he has fathered. Likewise, King Argaven of Karhide, although he fathered seven children, is especially fervent about giving birth to a child of his flesh even at great risk to himself because of his age. Is Le Guin saying that the mother-child relationship is stronger than the father-child's?

GENDER REDUX

Le Guin's recently revised article, "Is Gender Necessary? Redux" is her clear recognition of her flawed treatment of the gender in *The Left Hand of Darkness*. She tells me, "I wrote the original article in reaction against the kind of criticism that was bothering me very much because I was about to begin to agree with it; so I was quite defensive, and then my defenses broke down and I said, No, they are right. Estraven appears to be a man, I shouldn't have used the male pronoun. And then I revised the article."

ABOUT REVISIONS

"Have you ever considered revising *The Left Hand of Darkness*?" I asked her.

"I think that this would be almost impertinent. You have to let the whole work stand. You made a mistake, it's your mistake, then you go on and do better. I've had two opportunities to work on that. One is the short story directly related to *The Left Hand of Darkness*. I wrote it first then revised it for later publication."

The story she is talking about is "Winter's King," written about a year before *The Left Hand of Darkness*, and it concentrates on King Argaven of Karhide on Planet Gethen. In her first version of the story there is no mention of the ambisexual society. This idea came later and was incorporated in *The Left Hand of Darkness*. However, in response to the strong criticism of the use of male pronoun in the book, Le Guin revised "Winter's King," using the feminine pronoun for all Gethenians, while keeping the masculine titles such as King and Lord, to remind the reader of the ambiguity.

"The second opportunity I had was in the writing of the screenplay for *The Left Hand of Darkness*," she explained. "I've made up a pronoun. I referred to Gethenians not pregnant or in kemmer by the invented pronoun 'a' (pronounced "uh" [ ]) in the nominative case, 'a's' in the possessive case. I thought, 'Since it was to be used only for dialogues, you can do it without driving people mad.' You see, this is the main trouble with made-up pronouns, to read a whole novel with something in place of he or she is just not possible. Actually, they used to be the English genderless pronoun until the 17th or 18th century, when the grammarians declared the he was the generic, but it's quite arbitrary. In colloquial English we all still say, 'Anybody missing a notebook, will they stand up?' We say it all the time. But I couldn't refer to Estraven throughout the book as they. I did try to put in a made-up pronoun, but it leapt out of every sentence."

"Still, there are many times in the book that you wrote man or son, when you could easily have said people or children."

"Yes, over and over. There are many places I'd like to revise in that sense. I masculinized the book most unnecessarily. I agree with you. It gives me considerable pain now to see how easily I could have degendered it. But I feel a moral compunction about revising an old book."

"In this particular case, revision might well be a creative adventure," I suggested.

"It would be fun to try, I admit. The trouble is that the book has been in print ever since it was published; there has never been a time when it dropped out of print, when I could have done something about it."

INVENTED NAMES

"The name Ai, for the Envoy from Earth, carries triple meanings. But what about all the other invented names in the book?"

"No, they don't carry any meaning. They were picked purely for sound. Like a musical phrase."

"Except Argaven, maybe. I found him to be very aggravating."

She burst out laughing. "Oh, I never thought of it," she said in her sing-song voice." In Estraven people heard estrogen, which embarrasses me. Isn't that awful? Estraven is from Estre. So I thought, Estre-van, coming from Estre, what a pretty name, I liked the sound of it. It's purely aesthetic, my name making-up."

"Do you play music?"

"Well, not much, I played the recorder. But I've a musical daughter."

CRITICAL RESPONSE

"I was surprised to find so few reviews of *The Left Hand of Darkness*, a book which had won two major science fiction awards, in the mainstream press. Does the press ignore science fiction now as much as it used to?"

"Very nearly. The newspapers, if they review science fiction at all, tend to put it in a little corner called sci-fi, you know. Since 1969, when the book appeared, the academics are paying much more attention to science fiction. And we do get articles, some highly intelligent, some very academic, but they too appear only in very specialized publications. But just ordinary newspapers, no; science fiction is still ghettoized pretty consistently.

"What has also changed is that since the early 70s, when the whole English curriculum was opening up, many science fiction courses are taught in schools. High school teachers have discovered that science fiction is a wonderful way to get high school kids to read and talk about what they have read. The Russians discovered it long before we did; they have been using science fiction as a teaching device for decades."

"Does it bother you," I asked her, "that you are categorized as a science-fiction writer and thus excluded from what is generally considered 'literature'?"

"This is a very complicated issue," she said. "I object very strongly to the genrefication of literature. There is an assumption that everything called **genre** is secondary. This is simply untrue. Are writers such as Marquez, Borges, or Calvino automatically second-rate because they aren't writing realistic literature or mainstream fiction?

"On the other hand, there is marketing. In order to get the books to the interested public, libraries and bookstores and publishers need categories. And there is another aspect. As a writer of a despised **genre** , you have a kind of freedom. You are not nagged by the academics and critics, you can do whatever you please. In some ways I do feel trapped when I'm called a science fiction writer, and in other ways I feel delighted. On the whole, I think that boundary lines are changing, although conservative people don't want to admit it."

"Any advice for a young science fiction writer?"

"Read, and read the best. One doesn't have to have scientific knowledge. My science background is pretty minimal, but I was brought up to have a healthy respect for science, for I was a daughter of a scientist. If I need to know anything for my story, I go to the library and read about it. I think that most science fiction writers work this way.

"Science fiction begins at the moment where science ends, and then you can go on and build on what is known. Therefore, science fiction is getting more and more difficult to write because science develops so fast that the science-fiction writer has difficulty coping with it. This is one reason why there is less and less technological science fiction written because technology has overtaken it. It's different if you use social science, as I do, because social science is very slow moving and the writer is much freer."

IS LE GUIN ROMANTIC?

No doubt. If a political mission depends on a love relationship between two individuals, as is the case in *The Left Hand of Darkness*, Le Guin is certainly a romantic. We all know that this is not the way politics is done; that in reality human relationships are sacrificed for political goals. But as Le Guin writes in her introduction to the book, she deals with "what if," not with "what is." We are surrounded by "as is"; we need to speculate on alternatives that are rewarding and stimulating, even if they remain in the domain of "thought-experiment."

THEMES IN THE LEFT HAND OF DARKNESS

Le Guin's **themes** in *The Left Hand of Darkness* are many, complex, and interwoven.

The outer journey

An Envoy from Earth is sent to a distant planet in order to convince its people to join the League of the Planets for the purpose of sharing communication, knowledge, and trade. His adventures, misunderstandings, dangers, final awareness, and his singular relationship with one person of the planet Gethen (also called Winter) comprise the plot of the book.

Most science fiction books feature journeys, usually from Earth to different planets. At first glance, Le Guin follows suit. But further reading reveals that her journey consists of other journeys.

Journey within a journey

Ai's most important journey is not from planet Earth to planet Winter but his onerous and risky journey across the wastes of ice, together with Estraven, the native, the "Other." And this journey across the ice reflects another: Ai's true journey into himself. It is Ai's growing awareness of himself and of himself in relationship with the Other.

The outer and inner journeys

Ai's outer journey parallels his inner journey. "The seat of the soul is there," said the German poet Novalis, "where the outer and the inner worlds meet." And the American anthropologist Joseph Campbell said "that the laws of outer space are within us, that outer space and inner space are therefore one and the same thing."

Journey as symbol

The journey is one of literature's most prominent archetypal symbols, telling of man's journey through life. The journey, which is usually difficult and risky, is a learning experience, through which the hero-traveler searches for an answer to the meaning of life and to his own place in the world. By the end of the journey, the traveler gains maturity and self-awareness. It is a process of self-growth and self-discovery. One of the most famous journeys of antiquity, and one that has become a symbol for many others, in Homer's *The Odyssey*, in which Odysseus, triumphant after his conquest of Troy, travels for ten painful and arduous years to reach home, a **metaphor** for his soul and his anima.

Theme of love

One can read Le Guin's book as an unusual love story, even as the ultimate romantic love story of the space age, *Romeo and Juliet* in a sophisticated, space-age version. The lovers are not from feuding families but from different planets. They are aliens, foreign to, and different from, each other in every possible way-mentally, culturally, and even physically-yet they find the way to mutual understanding and true love.

Impossible love

In many ways, this is a tale of an impossible love, of love that transcends barriers and asserts itself in spite of its impossibility. The **theme** of love, mainly impossible-between brothers and between aliens-runs through the entire book, and underlies not only the Envoy's narrative but also the myths and legends of planet Winter.

The first impossible love is between brothers, specifically between Estraven and his brother Arek, that ends in the latter's suicide. The second impossible love is between two aliens, inhabitants of different worlds. This love too ends with death, possibly suicide. Is Le Guin's message that true love, even though unifying, is ultimately impossible and therefore tragic?

The self and the other

The **theme** of the Self and the Other runs parallel with the theme of love, because only love can bridge the chasm between aliens and turn the Self and the Other into I and Thou.

The concept of the Self and Other is a complex one. In *The Second Sex*, Simone de Beauvoir maintains that it is in the human nature of people to treat those who do not belong to their group as "others." "Otherness," she writes, "is a fundamental category of human thought," and "as primordial as consciousness itself." Thus, people from out of town are "strangers," those from other countries are "foreigners," and people from other planets would be "aliens." Likewise, states de Beauvoir in her philosophical treatise about the condition of women, men treat women as the "Other."

Central theme

The need to overcome this "otherness," to reach beyond it, to accept the Other wholeheartedly and to encompass the Other into the Self, is the central **theme** in *The Left Hand of Darkness*. Estraven and Ai are different from each other in every possible way. Although Estraven, the older, more experienced and educated of the two, has accepted Ai from the start, Ai, from Earth, has to go through an arduous process of education to be able to accept Estraven as a human being, as I and Thou.

I and Thou

I and Thou is the central **theme** in Martin Buber's philosophical treatise of the same name (1925; 2nd ed. 1958). True relationships are possible, he maintains, only when they are based on I and Thou and not on I and It.

New definition of love

In a way, Le Guin offers a new definition of love which does not call for the unification of the lovers, or for sexual consummation (an ironic comment on Freud's concept that sex is the basis of intimacy), but for total acceptance by each of the other person, with all his differences, as he is.

Gender

To create a planet whose inhabitants are ambisexual, men and women in one, is Le Guin's most original invention. She has taken one of the most poignant contemporary issues, that of equality between men and women, to the very extreme: when men and women become completely equal they become the same, they become menwomen, people who possess the qualities of both male and female.

Androgyny

The **theme** of androgyny (having the characteristics of both male and female) first appeared in ancient myths of both the East and the West as a symbol of completeness. Human life began as sexually undivided. In Plato's *Symposium*, Aristophanes tells the fable of angelic, eight-limbed creatures who threatened the gods and as a punishment were severed into two halves. Since then, the two halves, which consist of men and women, are frantically looking for each other in order to regain their unity. The biblical story is similar: God created Adam, one complete human being, and only later He created woman from Adam's own flesh. This division into male and female is the root of sexuality and its consequence is the expulsion from Paradise.

The **theme** of androgyny, or hermaphroditism, as a symbol of wholeness can be found in many myths. For the Chinese it is the assimilation of yin and yang expressed in the figure of a holy woman; the Zuni Indians make their chief god, Awonawilona, a he-she being; the Greeks make the son of the gods Hermes and Aphrodite, Hermaphroditus, unite in his body the physical characteristics of both sexes; and Eros, the god of erotic love, was both male and female. Hence, androgyny is connected in myth as well as in the human mind with yearning for completeness, for a state of Paradise.

Modern science has proven that both men and women carry male and female hormones, that the fetus is first neuter and only later becomes either male or female.

Unisex

Our contemporary society increasingly leans toward the unisex. Men and women not only wear similar clothes but are also encouraged to develop the qualities generally considered typical of the other sex: men to develop qualities such as gentleness, patience, love of peace, and the ability to nurture; and females to develop characteristics such as assertiveness and activeness.

Elimination of exploitation and war

Le Guin's unisex eliminates what Simone de Beauvoir considers woman's inferior status and exploitation as the "second sex." The results are intriguing: the elimination of sexuality as a social factor results in the elimination of exploitation and of rape on the individual as well as on the national level (rape of the environment, of natural resources, etc.), and the complete elimination of war.

Balance and wholeness

The implied message of *The Left Hand of Darkness* is that our lives would be greatly enriched if we, both men and women, were allowed to feel the entire range of human emotions and not be restricted to only some of them, the nature of which are dictated by tradition, prejudice, or misconception. In order to achieve peace and harmony in our personal life and in the world in general, we have to acknowledge and cultivate the female and male principles in each of us. Le Guin's manwoman idea is a **metaphor** for harmony, integration, and wholeness.

Balance and wholeness of the planet

Le Guin takes her idea of harmony between the male and female principles onto a national level: her planet Gethen reflects the integration of, and the balance between, the only two nations on the planet.

The first, Karhide, is anarchic, based on the female principle. In the revision of her essay "Is Gender Necessary?" Le Guin explains that "anarchy has historically been identified as female. The domain allotted to women-'the family,' for example-is the area of order without coercion, rule by custom not by force." Karhide's society is decentralized, flexible, and circular. Diametrically opposite is Orgoreyn, based on the male principle. There, people create "structures of social power," make laws and break them. Their society is centralized, rigid, and linear.

On Gethen the two societies are in balance. The story begins when this balance is dangerously threatened.

Taoism: holistic view of the universe

The Left Hand of Darkness embodies Le Guin's main belief, largely based on the ancient Chinese philosophy of the Tao (pronounced Dao), meaning "The Way." Since the 1960s, a decade known for its search for alternative ways of thinking and living, there has been a great interest in the West in Oriental philosophies such as Zen Buddhism and Taoism.

Taoism offers a holistic outlook of the way the universe works. "Tao is the course, the flow, the drift, or the process of nature," says Alan Watts in Tao: The Watercourse Way (1975).

While in other cultures light opposes darkness, good opposes evil, life opposes death, each one struggling to eliminate the other, in the Tao both light and darkness, good and evil, positive and negative are essential for the continuation of life. Opposites are seen as the two edges of one and the same pole, as north and south: you cannot have the one without the other. The two poles of cosmic energy-yang, positive, active, male, and yin, negative, passive, female-are essential for harmonious balance.

Taoism and psychology

Carl Jung explained Tao in the light of modern psychology: "If we take Tao as the method or conscious way by which to unite what is separated, we have probably come quite close to the psychological content of the concept." The value of Tao to modern psychology lies in its power to reconcile opposites on a higher level of consciousness, to reconcile in order to achieve a balanced way of living.

Taoism and The Left Hand of Darkness

The entire story of *The Left Hand of Darkness* strives toward the establishment of harmony and wholeness on the personal, national, and cosmic levels. The book begins with the disruption of the balance between the two countries of planet Winter, which is threatened with the eruption of the first war in its history. The two protagonists, citizens of different planets, are widely apart. From that point on the story moves toward restoring the balance and harmony between the protagonists, between the two countries on Winter, and between Winter and the rest of the universe.

CHARACTERIZATION IN THE LEFT HAND OF DARKNESS

Point of view

Le Guin presents her two **protagonists** from two limited points of view. The characters reveal their nature, first, through their own words and deeds. This is done by way of first-person narration. We learn much about Ai and Estraven through their own reports about themselves. They also reveal their nature through the impressions they make on each other. This way we obtain a double view of each character. But we do not have the writer's own view of her characters and can only guess at it. The development of the story mirrors the development of the relationship between the two protagonists, Ai and Estraven.

All other characters, such as King Argaven, his new Prime Minister Tibe, and some Orgoreyn officials, are minor characters who play their roles and then disappear from the story. They are largely flat, lacking in depth and complexity, and not fully characterized.

Ai And Estraven

In spite of all their differences, both Ai and Estraven share one basic characteristic: their utter loneliness. Ai, an alien from outer space, light years away from his own people and familiar environment, is physically and mentally different from all the people among whom he finds himself. Estraven, away from his family, from his country, is a fugitive in exile. Both are outsiders who are forced to take a long journey in a very inhospitable and cruel climate.

Genly Ai

His name, Ai, discloses his three roles in the narrative: as I, the narrator who sees everything from his own limited point of view; as Eye, the observer who learns to see into people and events; and as Ai, a cry of pain. The development of the character is his journey from I to Eye and at last to Ai, his final cry of pain as he comes full circle to the discovery of self and depth of soul.

Ai as I

Ai as I is a conventional, young, black Earthman, "confused and defensive," as Le Guin described him later, sent by the League of the Planets to the distant planet Gethen to convince them to join the interplanetary league. (The fact that Ai is black is mentioned but never really developed and one wonders why Le Guin saw the need to mention the color of his skin, It seems irrelevant and superfluous to the development of both the story and the character.)

Ai, who has volunteered for his mission, has given up his family and friends and the world he has known. He is a very dedicated and brave Envoy and although, as the story begins, he has already spent two years on the foreign planet with little success, he does not give up. He is determined to carry his mission to its hoped-for conclusion, whatever the consequences. When his two-year effort to persuade the King of Karhide fails, he moves on to the only other country on Gethen, ready to start working for his mission all over again.

But dedication and bravery are not enough. Ai, an average conventional Earth male, lacks the insight and understanding to carry out his mission. After two years on Gethen, he still does not understand its people, and is unable to step away from his conventional and Earth-like prejudices and accept people different from himself. In fact, although he is the alien on their planet, he regards the Gethenians as aliens. His main flaw is his inability to communicate and negotiate with the Gethenians and understand their way of thinking. In fact, he looks down on them: they are strangers, Others, different from himself.

Le Guin stresses time and again that what this Earth male finds so hard to accept is the feminine component of the Gethenians who are ambisexual, men and women in one. He prefers to relate to them as men, because this is the only way he knows, and whenever he detects any trait that he, the Earth male, considers feminine - and for this he selects mostly negative traits - he is disgusted. A Gethenian seems like a feminized man in his eyes when he detects his "fat buttocks that wagged as he walked, ... (his) soft fat face, and a prying, spying, ignoble, kindly nature." The inmates in the Labor Farm are repulsively effeminate because of their "gross, bland fleshiness, a bovinity without point or edge ... flabbiness and coarseness" and their trivial talk. (Is that how an Earth male regards women?) Likewise, Ai rejects Estraven, the Prime Minister and his only supporter, mainly because of his "soft supple feminity," his womanly performance "all charm and tact and lack of substance."

Ai as eye-less

At this point in the story, Ai, whose name suggests an "eye," is actually blind. He lets his prejudices get the better of him, causing him to misjudge what is actually happening around him to the point that he endangers his life and his mission without even being aware of it. In the beginning of the book he finds himself in the middle of a political intrigue that has a crucial bearing on his mission, and all he has to say is that he is bored. He listens to the state officials talk but, understanding nothing, he claims that "it's nothing to do with me" when it is all to do with him and his mission.

Ai's problem on Gethen is his accepting his situation as an alien, a stranger, a foreigner - "few foreigners are so foreign as I" - without making any real effort to understand these people who are foreign to him. He is an alien in the true meaning of the word. Away from his planet, his people, and his family, he is truly and utterly alone. The fact that he is at this point incapable of developing a close relationship with the Gethenians, or at least understanding them and thus feeling closer to them, not only causes him to feel completely forlorn but prevents him from carrying out his mission.

The trouble is that he does not yet understand his own mission, and therefore he keeps failing. Arrogantly and ignorantly, he declares that his mission is more important than personal relationships. He does not realize that his mission is also a personal odyssey. Ai is young, not yet thirty. He has yet to learn that his political mission - an alliance with Gethen - depends on his ability to overcome his alienation, establish true communication, and relate to the Gethenians on a personal level, on the level of his very being. His ability to learn to trust, care, accept the Other is the key to ending his isolation and to the success of his mission.

This becomes the real story: the education of Ai, the slow process of self-awareness, the process of becoming a full-fledged human being. Ai is the one character in the book who is undergoing a fundamental change and at the end of the book we meet a completely different person.

Ai as eye

Ai is too stubborn, ignorant, and blind to change on his own. Le Guin forces him to change by forcing him to be completely dependent on a Gethenian to whom he owes his life and with whom he has to spend many days in close proximity. Vulnerable and alone with Estraven on the ice, estranged from his sophisticated technology which enables him to contact his star ship, Ai is forced to open his eyes and see Estraven as he is, not a stranger, not an alien, but a human being, in all his strengths and weaknesses. For the first time Ai learns to share with Estraven what they have in common - their humanity - and at the same time accept their differences. Ai learns to accept Estraven's female component and, moreover, to confront and accept the feminine side in himself, the "gentle" part suggested by his first name, Genly. The profound love and understanding that develop between the two is possible not in spite of their differences but because of them; both learn to accept each other's "otherness." For love, Le Guin stresses again and again, is the acceptance of the Other, becoming "not We and They; not I and It; but I and Thou."

At this point Ai, having gained insight through his love for Estraven, also understands the true meaning of his mission. Only when he is able to love a Gethenian and establish real communication with him, can his mission to establish communication between the Planet Gethen and the rest of the planets be realized.

From Eye to Ai

Having gained love and lost it, Ai becomes a cry of pain and sorrow. The final chapter delineates how Ai has finally integrated the three meanings of his name: "I" the participant who becomes personally involved; "Eye" the observer who sees, understands and accepts; and "Ai" as a cry of pain.

Therem Estraven

The Gethenian **protagonist**, a manwoman, is portrayed from the very beginning in roles we are conditioned to see as male. He is a shrewd politician, a prime minister, a powerful aggressive figure, constantly pushing forward, struggling to realize what he strongly believes in. We never have the opportunity to see him in a traditional female role, mothering or nurturing, or even loving as a woman. In fact, when toward the end of the book he is going through his kemmering female phase, it requires a feat of the imagination to see him as a woman.

Compared with Ai, Estraven is a personality on a grand scale. To use Ai's words, Estraven possesses " a solidness of being, a substantiality, a human grandeur." Trained by the Handdara, a cult closely resembling Chinese Taoism, he is capable of great insight on the personal and political level. Thus he is the first and the only Gethenian to understand the crucial benefit that Ai's mission will bring to his country and his planet. Accordingly, he invests all his energy, his position, and later even his life, for the general good. And he is proven right, because his courage of conviction actually prevents Gethen from engaging in the first war in its history.

However, if this were all, he would have been a flat, one-dimensional character. In fact, he is a fully-rounded, multi-dimensional character who casts a long shadow, to use Le Guin's language, that reaches into the depth of the soul as well as to the depth of the Gethenian mythological past. Estraven's personal life, only suggested and never really described, has been steeped in profound and tumultuous human emotions, involving love and death, which feed his soul like a dark subterranean river.

Third point of view: first legend

In presenting Estraven's complex character, Le Guin skillfully offers a third point of view, that of Karhidish legends, which indirectly but very meaningfully, shed light on his life. The first legend, "The Place Inside the Blizzard," tells of two brothers who bore a child together and then vowed kemmering, meaning love and fidelity. But permanent kemmering between brothers is considered a great sin and is forbidden. Unable to bear the separation, one of the brothers commits suicide, which is an even greater sin that the first. Blamed for the suicide of his dead brother, the surviving brother is forced into exile.

As in the legend, we know that Estraven's brother, Arek is dead, that Estraven loved him deeply, and that he cannot free himself of this love. We also know that Estraven had been exiled from his village, apparently blamed for the suicide of his brother.

This is crucial to the understanding of Estraven's personality and to the development of the larger story. Because Estraven, as we later learn, is first attracted to the Envoy not for political reasons at all. When he first hears the name, Ai, he hears a human cry of pain. Much later in the story, when Estraven learns to communicate in mindspeech, he hears Ai's voice calling him from the depth of his soul in his brother's voice. Was it really his dead brother's cry of pain that Estraven heard in Ai's name that impelled him to help Ai's mission? Does it mean that Estraven actually sacrificed his career and later his life for personal reasons rather than for the good of his country? As in every complex personality, these questions are left unanswered.

This may be one of those impossible questions that the Handdara Cult maintains you learn not to ask.

Like Ai, Estraven changes through their relationship, though not as much. He, after all, being much more self-aware than Ai from the very start, has accepted Ai and related to him as a human being. (Is it because Estraven has self-awareness or because Ai reminds him of his dead brother?) But Estraven has to learn to let go of the past in order to be able and willing to love again.

This happens on the Gobrin Ice, when he finds himself alone with Ai, both stripped of outside resources. Here Estraven is, for the first time, on an equal footing with Ai; he, too, is now without the support of his own people. Only when they are alone, separated from all human society, its norms and regulations, can the two closely observe each other, learn to accept each other's weaknesses and differences, and each develop profound love for the other. Only then can both enter a relationship of "I and Thou."

Second legend

The second Karhidish legend, "Estraven the Traitor," tells of Estraven's ancestors, who were engaged in a life-and-death dispute over land. The tale ends happily, though, when the heirs of both feuding houses vow kemmering to each other and peace is established. However, the ancestor, also called Estraven, was labeled a traitor because he had traded land for peace.

This legend mirrors Estraven's present life on several levels. First, Estraven, the **protagonist** of our story, who, like his ancestors, also wants to trade land for peace, finally has to trade his life for the desired peace. Unlike the happy ending of the legend, the result is tragic for him.

Second, the word Traitor has a special significance to the personality of Estraven, and again, as with all else connected with Estraven, it works on several levels. He is accused of being a traitor by King Argaven for helping the Envoy from Earth and for wishing to preserve peace in Karhide, even at the price of giving up the disputed land. What is a Traitor for one, is a Hero for another.

The way Estraven ends his life presents a puzzling question. Is this, too, one of those questions which we have to learn not to ask? Skiing straight into the border-guards' guns, did Estraven commit suicide? Was another separation and exile from a loved one too much for him to tolerate? Or did he think that his death would help Ai to bring about the long-sought alliance of Gethen with the Ekumen and so deliberately sacrificed his life for a cause?

King Argaven

Of the few minor characters in the book, only King Argaven of Karhide is worth special attention, not so much for his personality as for the ideas he represents and for the comic possibilities he allows the writer. "The king is pregnant" is one of the most surprising sentences of the book. (Although Le Guin admits that she is fond of this sentence, it is not the reason she invented the ambisexual people of Gethen.)

A mad king ruling over a basically anarchic state is a comic figure. It seems that Le Guin is fascinated by the idea that the only ruler to reign over a nation of individuals who never "march in step" is a mad one. Le Guin's idea of anarchism is closely linked to her Taoist ideas that order is organic and should not be imposed. The Taoists recommend that a good ruler should rule as little as possible and leave his people alone. What ruler will agree to that unless he is light in the head? Le Guin, so it seems, pokes fun at our politicians, suggesting that the best politician is a mad one...

Everything about King Argaven is absurd. In the keystone ceremony it is he who labors to set the keystone in the arch while everyone else watches idly. Indeed, King Argaven is truly preposterous and aggravating. He laughs shrilly and at odd moments, baring his teeth and using four letter words freely-quite a clownish, silly figure, with little that is kingly about him.

The king is ruled by fears. He is afraid of everything and everybody, and so, he claims, he rules his country well. Being mad and fearful, he gives double messages which create confusion and are hard to follow. But this confusion and obscurity allow a nation of individuals to go on with their own lives with the least interference.

STRUCTURE AND STYLE IN THE LEFT HAND OF DARKNESS

Circular writing

The Left Hand of Darkness may not be an easy book to read for readers accustomed to linear writing. In linear writing the plot develops chronologically along a straight line. Le Guin's writing is anything but linear. It is circular or spiral and multi-leveled, making diversions and side-trips to the past, and further even, to ancient times, to myths and legends of her invented planet.

Multiple points of view

Increasing the complexity of the book is Le Guin's method of telling her story from multiple points of view. With each new chapter the readers must adjust themselves to another voice, to another teller of the story. In addition to the two alternating main narrators, a third narrator appears in one chapter, and in several others, the voice of the omniscient author takes over, recounting the legends and myths of Gethen.

To complicate the matter even further, sometimes each of the two narrators tells his own version of the same events and the same dialogues. Choosing to let both her **protagonists** narrate their version of the events and their observation of each other, Le Guin provides us with a subjective as well as an objective view of each narrator and of the events he is involved in. This enriches and deepens the narrative.

The plot becomes unduly complicated when Le Guin introduces, though only once, a third narrator, the only specifically female voice in the story. At that point many readers may become confused and even lost, not knowing who is speaking at any one time. Fortunately, as the story progresses, it narrows to only two narrators and becomes clearer and easier to follow.

Structure

The collage of first-person narratives, myths, legends, and scientific field notes creates a mixture that has drawn some harsh criticism for being mechanical and dogmatic. At the same time it has been hailed by other critics as presenting a remarkable unity, artfully illustrating the philosophical **theme** of the book, the Taoist holistic view of life, which requires the coexistence of opposites. It is not light or darkness, but always light and darkness. Likewise, it is the various parts of this collage which form the greater whole, just as in the story itself the different planets create the unity of the League of the Planets. In this way the structure of the book reflects its main theme.

Interconnectedness

The story develops through two different modes of writing: first, the first-person narrations telling the events as they unfold in the story's "present;" and second, the omniscient recounting of myths and legends of the far past. In the beginning of the book the two modes seem to run along parallel tracks; however, as the story develops, they overlap and it becomes clear that the myths and legends are there to provide background to the events of the story and to explain the psychology and philosophy of the people of Gethen. We can understand Estraven and his relationship to Ai only through consideration of the myths. Le Guin emphasizes the interconnectedness between the different modes of the narrative by using similarly named people and places in the main narrative and in the myths.

This interconnectedness between parts to create a greater whole exists in all of Le Guin's books, which together create a network of interconnectedness. Although each book or story is an independent entity, it is at the same time a part of the greater whole of her entire work, governed by a central **theme**: the relationship of all the invented planets in her different books to the League of the Planets. The suspense is always whether or not a certain planet will join, remain in, or leave the League. Rafail Nudelman points out that every Le Guin tale repeats "a movement from fragmentation toward unity." In the beginning of each story the hero finds himself in a fragmented world, a world of isolated enclaves amidst vast wastes. This recurring setting, maintains Nudelman, mirrors the League of the Planets which consists of isolated, independent entities of life in the vastness of the universe.

Recurring motifs

The recurrence of **themes** within the single work as well as throughout all her works reflects Le Guin's philosophical view that the universal structure is repeated in every entity small or large, and in every level of life: the micro and the macro reflect one another.

Chapter structures

Of the twenty chapters that comprise the book, half are told by Genly Ai, the Envoy from Earth, four by Estraven the Gethenian, one by a former female investigator from Earth; and five tell the myths and legends of the imagined planet. The first half of the book includes the myths and legends of Karhide, and the second half includes the myths and legends of Orgoreyn, the other country on Gethen.

What makes reading the first chapter something of a struggle is its magnitude of scope and multitude of ideas presented simultaneously, and in a rather static manner which obscures the story line. Although Le Guin begins with a wide base, as the story progresses, its plot and setting narrow. The first thirteen chapters serve as a long introduction to the real story which gains momentum and energy in the later part of the book. From Chapter 14 on, when we are left with only two characters struggling alone across a vast waste of ice, the story becomes clear and absorbing. At that point the story, characters, themes, and writing converge into a rich and harmonious unity; the narrative drive accumulates energy and the book displays the emotional density of the novel as a work of art.

Narrative technique

Genly Ai, the alien from Earth, writes most of the reports, but he also serves as the arranger of the different segments in the book, at a later time than the original writing. As a character, as the narrating "I," his story is fragmentary and subjective, his observations often mistaken, displaying ignorance and lack of insight. However, Ai, in the observant role of "Eye," and as the one who objectively arranges the parts and puts them together, offers a unified whole.

Juxtaposition of nature and man

Nature and its relationship to the characters are an essential **theme** in the book. In that, too, Le Guin is a faithful adherent of the Tao, which seeks its principles within nature and emphasizes the **metaphysical** foundations of nature, stressing harmony and balance. Man and nature are a unity. Man's fate is part of the function and the totality of the universe. The same principles that regulate nature also regulate man's life. Man can find peace only when he is completely attuned to the universe.

Ai, an alien on Winter, is constantly cold and is unable to adjust to the climate-a **metaphor** for his inability to understand and accept the Gethenians. He is foreign to their person, their environment, and their climate. So it is even more meaningful that it is on the Gobrin Ice, in bitter cold, that Ai learns to adjust himself, mentally and physically, to the cold planet and its inhabitants. It is when Estraven comments that Ai "sweats like one of us" that the ice between them begins to melt.

Nature, like all else in the book, reflects the tension between opposites, "silent vastness of fire and ice" that spells out in "black and white Death, Death" while "we laughed with joy."

Language

Le Guin is noted for using her language not only for functional reasons but with a care and precision that often approaches poetic beauty. This is unusual with science fiction writers whose plot and science fiction inventions often take precedence over their care for language. Specifically, Le Guin's description of landscapes is composed with a great amount of energy, a loving care for words and their sound.

Le Guin makes lavish use of **alliteration**, the repetition, at close intervals, of the initial consonant sounds as in bare bright or blinding biting, used to accentuate the poetry and the beauty of language, apart from the actual meaning of the words: "I felt a pang of pure pity for the man...sweating and superb under the weight of his panoply and power" (Chapter 3). In the same paragraph she also uses **assonance**, the repetition of vowel sounds: "gone now, down, done."

The beauty, precision, and rhythm of her language are manifested in the description of the landing of the long-awaited star ship in the final chapter:

She came down in a roar and glory, and steam went roaring up white as her stabilizers went down in the great lake of water and mud created by the retro; down underneath the bog there was permafrost like granite, and she came to rest balanced neatly, and sat cooling over the quickly refreezing lake, a great, delicate fish balanced on its tail, dark silver in the twilight of Winter.

This description, skillfully expressed in a single continuous sentence, lives up to the **climax** and excitement of the occasion, in some ways the ultimate goal of the story, the success of Ai's mission.

Some reservation

However, the beauty, richness, and precision of the language can present a problem: one finds it difficult to believe that Ai, a conventional stuffy young man, to use Le Guin's own expression, who throughout the book demonstrates shortsightedness and lack of understanding, is so skilled in the use of language and is capable of poetic insight. To be able to write so beautifully, one needs sensitivity and deep understanding of language and of life, something that Ai definitely lacks. This makes it difficult to believe in Ai's authenticity. Instead, one is constantly aware of Le Guin the writer who makes Ai speak for her, scheme her plot, and conjure up her ideas; this lends a feeling of affectation to the first half of the book. However, from Chapter 14 on, when Ai reaches a certain degree of maturity and becomes more sensitive and understanding, he and the language he uses coalesce.

Invented Names

Newly invented words and names foreign to our ears and eyes proliferate throughout the book and may make it difficult for the reader to follow the story line, especially in the first few chapters.

Of all the weird and hard-to-pronounce names of people, places, months, days, and new concepts, only the name of the Envoy, Ai, bears a meaning (triple meanings in fact), significant to the concept of the book. One wishes that the other names were also meaningful. It would have been easier to assimilate them and would have made the reading of the book more enjoyable.

Gender and language

It is inexplicable that Le Guin, who seems to excel in inventing new names and words, preferred to employ the conventional male pronoun in regard to her invented ambisexual people, the menwomen of planet Gethen. A rare chance to expand our language has been missed, and we are in dire need of expansion, especially in the area of gender. Now we muddy our writing with the clumsy "he or she" for lack of a pronoun for someone who is first and foremost a human being. Even wo/man or s/he could have served Le Guin's story better, for both words-woman and she-contain man and he, but neither man or he contains the female. Unfortunately, the use of the male pronoun has forever decided the fate of the Gethenians, at least in the mind of the readers, to be primarily male.

Fiction and science fiction

For years, science fiction has been a category of its own, avidly read by many, but basically separated from mainstream literature. It has been, for the most part, ignored by literary reviewers as well as by literary scholars, relegated to its own magazines, its own awards, and its own public. This has been a sore point for Ursula K. Le Guin, as it has been for every serious science fiction writer. Although since the publication of

The Left Hand of Darkness in 1969, and in many ways because of it, science fiction has been taken more seriously and even been a subject for academic studies, it is still largely an "alien" in mainstream literature.

In her introduction to *The Left Hand of Darkness*, Le Guin takes great pains to show that mainstream fiction and science fiction have much in common, and actually are basically the same; science fiction, contrary to what people may think, is not about the future but about the present, and like fiction, it reveals hidden truths about ourselves. It is not about different planets, it is about the present world.

Expanding the definition of science fiction

Le Guin is one of the first contemporary science fiction writers to have brought change to the **genre** and thus expanded the very definition of science fiction. For her, science fiction novels are an experiment in the imagination, "a thought-experiment." One of the essential functions of science fiction, she once wrote, is to ask provocative and essential questions which will reverse our habitual way of thinking. Science fiction presents "questions, not answers."

Instead of accepting reality as given and unchangeable, the science fiction writer explores it in the laboratory of the imagination, turns it upside down and inside out, searching for its inner truth.

Truth-lies-imagination

How is it possible, she asks, that lies-characters, places and events that have never existed-can tell us the truth about ourselves?

Le Guin is examining the words truth, imagination, and lies, and intentionally equates and confuses that which is unreal, invented, or imaginative, with lies. And so, in a seemingly absurd way, her story - meaning her imaginative, fictional world that does not exist in reality - is a lie that illuminates the truth about reality and about ourselves.

In that way, both mainstream fiction and science fiction tell the truth about reality through "lies," that is, through imagination. "Truth is a matter of the imagination," says Le Guin through her **protagonist** in the very beginning of *The Left Hand of Darkness*.

Fiction as metaphor

Both fiction and science fiction, continues Le Guin in her analysis of the similarity between the two genres, are metaphors-imaginative word-pictures that provide a complex of associated meanings. The main difference is that science fiction draws its **metaphors** from science and technology. As for "the future," this, too, is a **metaphor**, which means that "the future" of science fiction is not really the future but the present.

Metaphors of science and technology

One wonders whether what Le Guin considers a minor difference between fiction and science fiction, namely, **metaphors** drawn from science and technology, is responsible for the fact that many people, otherwise avid fiction readers but who feel that science and technology are foreign languages to them, **refrain** from embarking on these journeys to imaginary worlds.

Fear of the future

Fear of the future, of the unfamiliar, of change, may be another reason, not addressed by Le Guin, which explains why some readers avoid reading science fiction. Reality may not be perfect, but at least it is familiar. Most people tend to resist change and fear the unknown.

Science fiction offers alternatives outside the reader's realm of experience. If mainstream fiction offers exploration into the known, science fiction offers exploration into the unknown, and the androgynous society of Gethen in *The Left Hand of Darkness* is the unknown. The reader may not be able to identify with the Gethenians, who are at once men and women, having no idea how a manwoman feels or thinks.

In this respect, science fiction presents us with territories and experiences in which we find ourselves alien. It is not only about aliens, but it also turns us, the readers, into aliens in a strange land. Moreover, science fiction suggests the possibility of a change; the future may be far different from the present. We all aspire to a better world in which wars and rapes will be eliminated. Still, the ambisexual society of Gethen is not our society, and the reader may become impatient, feeling that we should learn to deal better with our present problems, such as rape and wars. The literature of "as if" may be wonderful, but after all we live in "as is."

The good news for fiction readers who are now about to read *The Left Hand of Darkness* is that it has more to do with human relationships than with science and technology, more with "software" than with "hardware."

THE LEFT HAND OF DARKNESS

TEXTUAL ANALYSIS

CHAPTER 1: A PARADE IN ERHENRANG

The first chapter introduces us to the major characters of the novel and to some of the unique features of the new planet Gethen (Winter), while delineating the main **themes** of the book. The complexity of its ideas, coupled with an abundance of strange and difficult-to-pronounce names, makes this chapter somewhat difficult to read.

POINT OF VIEW

This is the first of ten chapters (out of twenty) in which the **protagonist** (the main character), an Envoy from Earth, tells his own story and reports the events from his point of view. This technique of first-person narration limits our perception to what the narrator knows.

UNITY AND HARMONY

Genly Ai, the narrator, tells of a royal ceremony which takes place in Erhenrang, the capital city of the kingdom of Karhide. This ceremony consists of the mounting of the keystone which will unite the two piers and complete the arch of Rivergate. This is a central symbol in the book. In a way, the movement of the entire book is from fragmentation toward unity and wholeness, an idea reflected by the mission of the Envoy from Earth: to unite the planet Gethen with the League of the Planets for coordination and harmony in the universe.

The keystone is set in pink mortar. In olden times the mortar was mixed with human blood and bones; now it is mixed with animal blood-blood being necessary for bonding. Does this mean that in order for Genly Ai to bring about the bonding between the planets, blood will have to be spilled? Is that why the color red is so prevalent in the book?

PLURALITY

True to Le Guin's philosophical beliefs based on the Chinese philosophy of the Tao, unity and harmony do not mean uniformity or unification but the sum of opposites. The country of Karhide, one of only two countries on planet Gethen, is based on plurality. When the people and dignitaries march, each marches to his own rhythm. There is no attempt to march in step. The result is not confusion and disharmony, as we, schooled in Western tradition, may expect, but human dignity, the dignity which results from respect for individuality.

Likewise, the music that accompanies the parade is "discordant," with each band playing its own music. Not unity, but a cacophony of sounds and rhythms. "Karhide is not a nation," explains Estraven, "but a family quarrel."

Ironically, in this anarchic society of individuals, it is the Envoy from Earth who, feeling lonely, craves "sameness," wishing "to be like everybody else." The melange of individuals around him only adds to his sense of physical alienation.

UNITY BASED ON PLURALITY

Both unity and plurality create the ironic political government of Karhide, which, contradictory in terms, is anarchistic monarchy, an anarchy governed by a king. But Le Guin's world, just as that of the Tao, is made up of the coupling of contradictions, of the bridging of polarities. In the traditional keystone ceremony, it is the king who works to set the stone in mortar, while the people watch idly.

What kind of king can rule over anarchy? Only a mad king. Were he sane, he might wish to do away with the anarchy and establish his reign. And so the King of Karhide is insane. To ensure his madness, the musicians play him the royal music, which is a discordant blast that would drive any one mad.

CHARACTERS: GENLY AI

The Envoy from Earth, who narrates the events and his feeling about them, is young, honest, and naive. He honestly reports whatever he observes and hears. But because he is a naive and undeveloped young man, he sees much but understands little. His narration reveals more than he is conscious of. It is up to us, the readers, to interpret his words.

Although Genly Ai has been on planet Gethen close to two years, still he does not understand its people. Ironically, he has remained very much a stranger not only because the Gethenians regard him as an alien, but also because he sees them as aliens and strangers. He is so entrenched in Earth standards and **conventions** that he is incapable of accepting the Gethenians as they are-different from him. Judging them by Earth criteria, he is unable to extend himself, transcend his preconceptions, and accept that which is the Other.

His inability to accept the Gethenians is all the more ironic because to bring them into the alliance of the planets is the very reason he has traveled from Earth to Gethen. How does he plan to bring about this alliance based on communication, harmony, and coordination, if he, the Envoy, looking down on them because they are so different from him, is unable to relate to them as human beings? Ai's flaw is that he has taken his mission literally-political alliance - and not metaphorically-spiritual alliance. Moreover, he tries to communicate with Karhide as a nation and to deal with its authority, as one would have done on Earth. But Karhide is a country of individuals, "not a nation but a family quarrel" and the only way to communicate with its people is through individuals. The result is that he has stayed on the planet for two years without accomplishing his mission.

Ai is blind to the truth, which is, as he himself says at the outset of this chapter, "a matter of the imagination." But instead of using his imagination to gain insight into the Gethenians' psyche, he is stuck in the facade of things. Twice in this chapter he fails to read correctly what will later prove extremely significant to him and his mission, instead dismissing what he sees as boring and having nothing to do with him.

In no other issue are his preconceptions and misunderstanding so pronounced as when it comes to the matter of gender. He cannot see the Gethenians as they really are: people who are at once man and woman. In fact, Ai mistrusts the Gethenians exactly because of this wholeness.

Thinking of Estraven as male, for instance, Ai finds his womanly side not only confusing but somehow false, making him seem inconsistent and untrustworthy. He sees the inherent female in Estraven as mostly negative, the way many males regard effeminate men on Earth: lacking in substance, being deviant, and engaging in intrigues. The Gethenian face seems to him to be as incomprehensible as the face of a cat, a seal or an otter.

Ai also fails to understand shifgrethor, the most significant social principle in Karhide. Shifgrethor, which guides the way all Gethenians behave toward each other, includes the concepts of "prestige, face, place, and pride-relationship." It is a difficult concept that Le Guin has invented and it requires further reading to fully understand it.

ESTRAVEN

The Prime Minister of Karhide, on the other hand, displays "human grandeur"; he is a man of moral substance, according to Ai's report. Nevertheless, Ai mistrusts him for the same reason he mistrusts all Gethenians-for displaying feminine traits.

This is ironic because Estraven is the only person in Karhide who has taken Ai and his mission seriously. He has investigated the Envoy and his space ship as well as the validity of the mission, and he is determined to further Ai's cause.

Estraven's grandeur of soul is seen in his humane handling of the land dispute between Karhide and its neighbor, Orgoreyn, the only other country on the planet Gethen. In order to prevent bloodshed, Estraven, acting alone and at great risk to himself, helped some farmers to resettle across the old border. Estraven is ready to give up the disputed land rather than let people be killed. He stresses that he does not serve any one, not even the king; he serves higher causes and higher ideals.

TIBE

The King's cousin, Tibe, has his eye on Estraven's position as Prime Minister. He is the master of intrigue, scheming to bring about drastic changes in the planet: to turn the anarchy in Karhide into dictatorship under his leadership, and to introduce war into Gethen's 13,000 years of history without wars. Tibe understands that Estraven, who exchanges land for peace, and the Envoy from Earth, who advocates alliance and harmony among planets, are his mortal enemies.

POINT OF VIEW

This chapter is told in the first person, by Ai in his role as "I," who reports about the events. Only later will he serve in his other capacity, not yet developed, as "Eye," the observer. It is ironic that he reveals about himself much more than he himself realizes. At this point, self-awareness is not his strongest point.

CHAPTER STRUCTURE

The chapter is divided into two parts, or two locations. First, the celebration of the keystone, in which Ai displays his ignorance and inability to grasp the politics and the social order around him. Second, at Estraven's home, Ai displays his inability to understand the one person in all Karhide who respects his mission and who treats him like a human being. It is Ai, the alien, who treats Estraven as the stranger.

WORDS

Le Guin takes great care with words. Not only does she make every word tell, but also makes every word act on several levels. Take for instance the word "yellow," a dominant color in this chapter. During the keystone ceremony Ai experiences physical warmth for the first time on planet Winter, with its sub-zero temperatures and permanent snow. During this spiritual ceremony, the sun shines bright and warm, signifying enlightenment, inspiration, and goodness. Is it a hint that once Ai's mission is successfully completed, he, who is always cold, will feel warmer?

Le Guin whimsically turns words inside out, questioning basic concepts. Patriotism, for example, which for the Envoy from Earth means love for one's homeland, is for Estraven, and clearly for Le Guin, "the fear of the other," and fear of the "other" - of the alien, of the one different from us - is a key **theme** of the book.

THE LEFT HAND OF DARKNESS

TEXTUAL ANALYSIS

CHAPTER 2: THE PLACE INSIDE THE BLIZZARD

A TALE OF LOVE

At first reading, this chapter seems a surprise and an irrelevant detour from the narrative. Only later it turns out to be directly connected with one of the central **themes** of the book; a story of love between two brothers. This is love in its negative form; love prohibited, and love betrayed. It is the tale of starcrossed brothers, whose vow to stay together is broken by the complex code of incest. The result is tragic; one brother commits suicide and the other is banished from his village. When the exiled brother meets his dead brother in the place inside the blizzard, the latter cannot speak his brother's name.

TECHNIQUE

As strange and as disconnected as this chapter may seem, every detail will recur and play a significant part in later chapters.

This is characteristic of Le Guin's method of composition; a mosaic of self-references and of recurring themes.

STRUCTURE

"The Place Inside the Blizzard" is the first of a series of Gethenian legends and myths that Le Guin interweaves with her story of the Envoy on the planet Gethen. These tales create the mythology and culture of the planet, endowing it with depth and history. Thus the story unfolds on multi-levels, constantly employing references and **allusions** between the present of the planet and its past.

This multi-level structure reflects Le Guin's philosophy of life as developing in a spiral form. Events that happened in the past repeat themselves again and again in numerous variations. Whatever happens is neither disconnected nor accidental, but has deep roots in the past.

STYLE

The language of this chapter is that of legends; short on details and explanations, containing minimal but essential dialogue; nothing extraneous to the important story line is presented.

At the ending of the chapter, as is often so in legends, harmony is re-established; the disorder in the nature of the world is corrected and the usual order of life is resumed; the living brother takes back his curse - "his name and his shadow" - and his old village prospers once again.

THEME 1: TWO BROTHERS

In *The Uses of Enchantment* (1976), Bruno Bettelheim writes that the theme of two brothers is very prevalent in fairy tales, and is central to one of the oldest of them, found in an Egyptian papyrus of 1250 BC. According to one study there are at least 770 different versions of the theme.

In the "two brothers" tales one brother usually stays home and the other sets out on an adventurous quest. The brothers keep in touch through magic. The two brothers actually reflect the two sides in human nature, the desire to stay home, safe and attached to the past, and the urge to reach out to the future. The stories often teach that to live completely attached to the past is stunting; while it is safe, it allows no life of one's own. Only the integration of the two can lead to a successful existence. We will see this **theme** resurface throughout *The Left Hand of Darkness*.

THEME 2: LOVE FORBIDDEN AND BETRAYED

Although incestuous love is not forbidden on Gethen, it can last only until one of the brothers gives birth to a child because permanent incestuous bonding is forbidden. In this story, the two brothers swore eternal love, kemmering, to each other and thus defied the law of the planet.

The living brother feels deeply betrayed by his brother, who committed suicide rather than escape to the south where they might have lived together in anonymity.

On the planet Gethen, suicide is considered a worse sin than murder, although Le Guin offers no explanation for this law. When one of the brothers gave birth to a child, the two were commanded to separate. Unable to comply, one of the brothers committed suicide, defying the law of the land.

THEME 3: LEFT HAND

The dead brother seizes the living brother by his left hand causing it to freeze and later to be amputated. The significance of the left and right hands as well as of the title of the book becomes clearer later, specifically in Chapter 9, the second legend of Karhide, and even more so in Chapter 16.

BIBLICAL REFERENCE

When the exiled brother finally managed to find a place where no one knew him, he assumed a new name; Ennoch. This is a clear reference to E'noch, Cain's son (Genesis; 4, 17). The Biblical tale of the two brothers Abel and Cain is a tale of betrayal. Both tales result in the death of one brother and the exile of the other. The living brother is forced to be "a fugitive and a vagabond" (Genesis; 4, 14) hunted by all. In the Bible, Cain complaints to God, who grants him a special mark to protect him. Finding peace he settles and fathers a son, E'noch. The living brother in Le Guin's story, blamed for the suicide of his brother, becomes nameless and gains peace by assuming a new name, Ennoch.

CENTRAL IMAGE

The place inside the blizzard is a certain spot on the glacier in the northern country, windless, snowless, and shadowless, where the two brothers, the living and the dead, meet for the last time. This scene recurs in a different version in Chapter 19, when it assumes its full meaning.

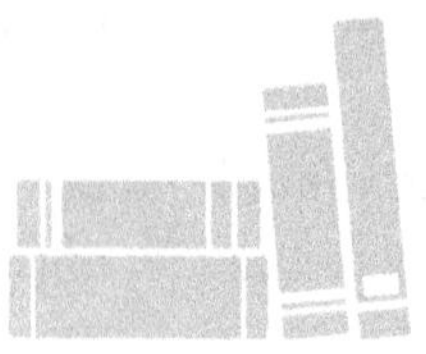

THE LEFT HAND OF DARKNESS

TEXTUAL ANALYSIS

CHAPTER 3: THE MAD KING

POINT OF VIEW

The third chapter, like the first one, is written from Ai's point of view. He reports the progress of his long-sought-for audience with the king of Karhide in order to discuss with him his mission: bringing Gethen into the Ekumen, the League of the Planets. (Ecumenicism is a movement to unite the followers of different religions or beliefs.)

THEME OF BETRAYAL

As in the former chapter, the **theme** of betrayal features prominently. The king accuses Estraven, his Prime Minister and a firm supporter of the Envoy, of betraying his country by advocating that Karhide give up certain disputed land, and that it join the League of the Planets. The King declares Estraven a traitor and orders him exiled.

The **theme** of betrayal acquires an additional twist when the King tells Ai that it is Estraven who has betrayed him by advising the King not to meet with Ai but to send him away. Ai, who has no insight into the people of Karhide or their politics, is rightly confused.

CHARACTERIZATION: THE KING

The chapter heading informs us that the King is mad. The best king to rule an anarchic country of individuals, says Le Guin, is a mad king. The Chinese philosophy of Taoism, which underlies much of Le Guin's thinking, advises rulers to stay out of people's way, to govern as little as possible, and to let people alone. Only a mad king will agree to be as little of a king as possible. Otherwise he may begin to exercise his authority and turn the country into a dictatorship. And in fact, the King, under the influence of his cousin, the intriguing and power-seeking Tibe, is on the point of turning the country into a centralized state with its characteristics of national aggression and wars.

King Argaven is neurotic, prone to fits of anger, full of fears, and generally very aggravating. He seems unstable, confusing truth with lies, and is unable or unwilling to understand Ai's mission. He behaves more like an immature, fearful, and irresponsible child than a serious ruler.

CHARACTERIZATION: GENLY AI

This is the first stage in the education of the Envoy, a main **theme** of the book. Failing to communicate with the King, and with his only supporter, the Prime Minister Estraven, in exile, Ai finally understands that he cannot achieve his mission through the King and the ruling authority of Karhide. In fact, he may have lost his chance of getting the planet Gethen to join the Ekumen. He is overwhelmed by a feeling of failure, but for the first time he is willing to take the initiative in learning more about this strange planet.

Moreover, if truth is a matter of the imagination, as Ai says in the first chapter, for the first time Ai is using his imagination to gain some insight into the real Estraven. While imagining the proud Prime Minister trudging his way on foot into exile, Ai, for a short time at least, has a glimpse of Estraven as a human being, a person in trouble and in pain. Through this act of empathy with the "other," Ai finally understands that Estraven has been trying to warn him of the danger he, Ai, is in, advising him to leave the court and the city.

STRUCTURE AND BACKGROUND

The audience with the king allows Le Guin the space and justification to provide the story with the necessary background. Through the Envoy's explaining his mission to the king, Le Guin explains to her readers the function and the history of the Ekumen (communication, harmony, and sharing of knowledge), the differences between the people on Earth "who come in all colors" (we learn now, for the first time, that Ai is black), and the Gethenians who are "yellow-brown or red-brown," and mainly about the all-important difference of gender.

GENDER

From Ai's conversation with the king we also learn about the peculiar nature of the Gethenians: they are ambisexual or androgynous, meaning, they are not divided into two sexes, they are neither men nor women, but each is both man and woman in one. The Gethenians are sexually neuter and inactive except for four days a month, when they are in kemmer, that is, sexually active. Only then, and for these few days, do they become male or female sexual beings.

When the King, looking at photos of people from other planets, asks Ai to explain to him what a woman is, Ai, for lack of a Karhidish word for woman, uses a word for a female animal in heat.

Once again Le Guin stresses the fact that Ai, the Earthman, rejects the Gethenians for the feminine aspects of their nature. And whenever he detects a feminine trait in the King's behavior, it is always negative. The King laughs "shrilly like an angry woman," or he is sullen "as an old she-otter in a cage."

IRONY

Seen from the king of Karhide's eyes, people on Earth who are permanently sexually defined as men or women are "perverts," "disgusting," and "monstrously different." It is ironic that what we have always taken for granted and natural is not to be taken for granted at all. This is Le Guin's way of questioning what we have always assumed to be solid facts: definable male and female identities.

COLOR RED

In this chapter the color red carries a special significance: it alludes to the blood necessary for bonding. The King's Hall is all red and so are the drapes. The drapes are worn out with time, reminding us of the blood that has been used for mortar. Things are not what they used to be and the red has lost much of its vigor, a clear **allusion** to the deteriorating state of affairs in Karhide.

SCIENCE FICTION

Le Guin introduces here two of her science fiction concepts: (1) A sophisticated communication device called the ansible, one of the very few hardware inventions Le Guin uses in her book. The ansible can transfer a message to distant planets the moment it is written. (2) Timejumping. From H.G. Wells' The Time Machine (1895) on, the question of time has always fascinated science fiction writers and presented them with the challenge of mastering it and devising ever more sophisticated means to transport man through many light years, to the farthest planets, and back to Earth. Le Guin does not linger much on the question of time (although she does dwell on inner mental time, as we will see from the Gethenians' peculiar calendar), but she does feel the need to explain rationally how the Envoy from Earth has experienced the many years needed to travel to Gethen and still remained young. She calls it "timejumping" and uses the hypothesis that if we travel as fast as light we do not age.

THE LEFT HAND OF DARKNESS

TEXTUAL ANALYSIS

CHAPTER 4: THE NINETEENTH DAY

A second Karhidish legend: this, like the earlier one, seems on first reading to be unrelated to the narrative. However, it prepares us for Ai's meeting with the Foretellers, the Karhidish version of divinators, in Chapter 5.

IMPOSSIBLE QUESTIONS

This tale serves to demonstrate how futile and dangerous impossible questions are. Lord Berosty insists on asking the Foretellers an impossible question: to name the day of his death. The clever answer that the Foretellers give him - that he will die on the 19th day of any month-drives him into sheer misery and madness.

THEMES OF LOVE AND BETRAYAL

Lord Berosty's love companion, Herbor, is ready to sacrifice his life to obtain the desired answer and thus restore his friend's peace of mind. But Lord Berosty, unsatisfied with the second answer - that he will live longer than Herbor - kills Herbor with a "red stone." Is blood necessary to complete the bonding between lovers? Only after he has killed his faithful friend does Lord Berosty hold the dead man as if the two were in "kemmer and all was well."

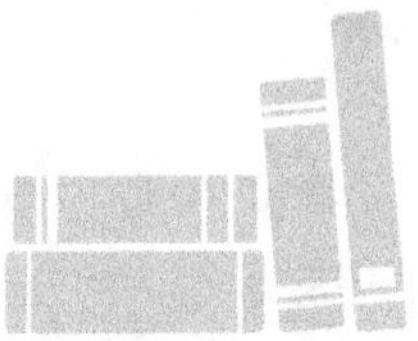

THE LEFT HAND OF DARKNESS

TEXTUAL ANALYSIS

CHAPTER 5: THE DOMESTICATION OF HUNCH

POINT OF VIEW

This is Ai's third first-person report telling of the progress of his mission.

AI'S EDUCATION

The first stage in Ai's education on Gethen is to leave the capital of Karhide, the seat of government, and gain some knowledge and understanding of the country's ancient religion, the Handdara. It seems that Ai knows much about the external life of the Karhidish but very little about their spiritual life. Now he undertakes a long journey to meet the Foretellers, sage and enlightened people well trained in the Handdara. With their help, Ai slowly begins to grasp that understanding means to go beyond what one knows and to be receptive to different and unfamiliar ways of thinking.

THE HANDDARA CULT

The Handdara cult is introversive, dark, passive, and silent. It is the ideal religion of the individual: it has no institution, no priests, no hierarchy, no vows, no creed. And, Le Guin adds sarcastically, it may not even have a God. This is Le Guin's way of indirectly criticizing our institutional religions, in which the individual becomes lost in the multitude.

The Handdara cult embodies the holistic vision of the Tao. One of its principles is that there are no real answers except the one that we all die. One has to accept his own limitations, to understand that the only certainty is death, and that it is only uncertainty that makes life possible.

At the same time, if one accepts one's own limitations and the knowledge that there are no ultimate answers, and limits oneself to a concrete yes-and-no question, he may benefit from the special divination ability of the Foretellers. Having learned how dangerous an impossible question is, from the tale of Lord Berosty, Ai asks the Foretellers a limited question: Will Karhide join the Ekumen within five years? He receives a definite answer: yes.

PRESENCE

The essence of the Handdara religion is the discipline of Presence, something like trance or untrance, self-loss or self-augmentation, which is extreme sensual awareness.

TIME

Because it is Presence, rather than Progress, that matters, the Gethenians live permanently in Year One, meaning, in the very present. It is the Now which counts, and therefore the current year is always Year One. Now we can understand better the implications of the tale of Lord Berosty, who, instead of immersing himself in the discipline of Presence and living in Year One, insisted on knowing the unknown, the day of his death. By being obsessed with the unknown future he lost his present and his Presence.

COEXISTENCE OF OPPOSITES

Here again we meet the Chinese philosophy of Taoism. It is never either light or darkness, as is the case in Western culture, but light and darkness together which create the whole and which are both necessary for the world to exist. Opposites do not negate, contradict, or battle each other; they are integral to each other and each exists because of the other. Just as we cannot separate north from south without eliminating both, so is the case with light and darkness, good and evil. Likewise, the Foretellers go into darkness in order to see light and gain enlightenment. Moreover, one can understand something only through the knowledge of its opposite: trance and untrance, activity and inactivity, movement and motionlessness, learning and unlearning. Ai has to unlearn much of what he had learned on Earth in order to understand the habits and culture of the planet of Gethen.

PRESENCE VERSUS PROGRESS

Le Guin introduces some science fiction hardware as a means of commuting: landboats, very slow trucklike vehicles that can travel on land and water. But her main purpose - and this characterizes her whole approach to science fiction writing-is not to surprise the reader with a brilliant technical invention but to embody an important idea. Here she is very critical of the fast pace in which we, on Earth, conduct our lives, and offers her philosophy of "presence": Presence, rather than progress, is what really matters. The Karhidish are never in a hurry and mostly go on foot, having neither horses nor airplanes. Their vehicles move slowly, about 25 miles an hour, very slowly by our Earth standard. Yet Le Guin hails their slowness as a more natural and humane way to live. In her essay "Is Gender Necessary?" she explains that the Gethenians "do not rape their world. They have developed a high technology, heavy industry ... but they have done so very slowly, absorbing their technology rather than letting it overwhelm them." Their progress represents not only sensitivity to their ecology but also a balance between male and female traits: aggressiveness and pushing forward, on one hand, and patience, on the other.

WAR

One of the most interesting aspects of planet Winter is its lack of war. Although the Gethenians have their share of fights, aggressiveness, murders, and other abominable crimes, they are expressed on a personal level, and they never lead to war. Le Guin's explanation is intriguing: because they are a nation of individuals (they behave "like animals ... or like women," Ai explains) they lack the ability to mobilize; theirs is more like "a family quarrel," not like a national war. Le Guin believes that order can be more effectively achieved through rituals and parades than by armies or police.

Le Guin cannot escape injecting her sarcasm, with an eye to our society: if the Gethenians become patriotic, they will have "an excellent chance of achieving the condition of war."

GENDER

Le Guin is clearly having fun with her invention of the wo/man being, and humorously opens her chapter with "My landlady, a voluble man." What incites Ai, the typical Earth male, to regard his landlord as a woman? Certain unpleasant physical characteristics: his fat, wagging buttocks, his soft, fat face, and his "prying, spying, ignoble, kindly nature."

COLOR RED

In this chapter, too, the color red appears: the Towers are "blood-red"; even the needles of the most common tree on the planet are pale-scarlet; "everything is red and brown."

STYLE

Le Guin arrives at her best writing whenever she describes, or rather invents, landscapes embedded in eternity. Hers is a language of vastness and of timelessness, of great precipices, boundless lands and huge white shadows. In contrast, "a tiny string of dots," the landboats, creep thousands of feet below. But even in the midst of this dramatic scenery Le Guin is compelled to allude to the deplorable state of nature on Earth: Unlike Earth, here in Karhide, where people are aware of ecology, the woods are carefully tended. The only difficulty with these poetic and beautifully described landscapes is to believe that Ai, the narrator, this young and naive person from Earth, could actually write them. He seems anything but poetic.

CHARACTERIZATION

Ai, as a typical Earth man, tries to understand the Foretellers' "business" rationally, and calls it "chance," using Earth's rationale and terms. But this does not work. Rationalization is not the way to gain truth or insight. Only after his profound experience with the Foretellers, which he translates to Earth's terms and calls "the domestication of hunch," does Ai begin to sense some of life's openness and possibilities. One does not have to know the future. But it must be open to countless possibilities.

IRONY

Le Guin treats with **irony** the differences between the state of affairs on Earth and on Karhide. Speaking of prediction, Ai has doubts of the ability of the Foretellers to predict the future. After all, he reasons, throughout the history of man we have had "God speaks, spirits speak, computers speak."

Later, he understands that the Foretellers' act is not so much a prophecy as an observation, that they have managed to "domesticate the hunch," the human and natural insight into the working of the world, while on Earth they are too busy with technology, such as "NAFAL ships and instantaneous transmission."

THE LEFT HAND OF DARKNESS

TEXTUAL ANALYSIS

CHAPTER 6: ONE WAY INTO ORGOREYN

POINT OF VIEW

Now Le Guin introduces a new first-person narration, that of the demoted Prime Minister, Estraven. He tells of his desperate attempt to cross the border of Orgoreyn, the other country on Gethen. Pursued by his rival, the new Prime Minister, Tibe, Estraven can barely make his escape.

THEME OF LOVE AND BETRAYAL

For the first time we get a glimpse into Estraven's personal life. His consort of ten years, Ashe, offers to accompany him into exile, but Estraven is bitter and angry and accuses him of breaking their oath three years earlier. Regarding his life "like a broken promise," Estraven chooses to go into exile alone.

POLITICAL OPPOSITES

Planet Gethen is divided between two countries ruled by opposite regimes. While Karhide, although ruled by one mad king, is anarchic, Orgoreyn, ruled by a government of thirty-three official Commensals, is totalitarian, with an active secret police and an inspector lurking behind every man. This political setup corresponds to Le Guin's philosophy of the coexistence of opposites. As long as the balance between the opposite sides holds, peace reigns. The trouble begins when one country, in this case Karhide, led by the new Prime Minister, Tibe, is on the verge of changing its anarchic regime of a thousand years to become centralized and efficiently ruled like Orgoreyn.

CHARACTERIZATION: ESTRAVEN

Estraven is a clever and shrewd politician. Although he has lost his power at home and is in exile, he is far from being helpless. He is constantly scheming to realize his vision.

Questioned by two of the ruling party of Orgoreyn, Estraven offers a clear analysis of the current political situation (the land dispute, Tibe's intrigues and drive to change the political situation and the balance of powers) and the result is imminent danger to both countries. He tells them about the Envoy and his mission, and with profound and visionary insight adds that the Envoy heralds a new era in which the regimes of both countries will have to change: "he brings the end of Kingdom and Commensalities with him in his empty hands."

"Why?" they ask and Estraven explains that in order to deal with the strangers of eighty worlds, all the Gethenians will have to unite and be friends. Estraven manages to persuade the

Orgoreyn regime to permit the Envoy to enter their country and present to them his mission.

STYLE

There is a definite difference between the way Ai and Estraven narrate their stories, even though the difference may be not easy to define. It stems from their different personalities and lies in the tone of the narration. Ai is young, naive, and inexperienced, while Estraven is older, powerful, and experienced in the ways of the world and of the heart. The tone of Estraven's narration reflects his confidence and his moral conviction. His language is more elegant, and richer, as for example, "I had gone all to grease and luxury and had lost my wind for walking."

THE LEFT HAND OF DARKNESS

TEXTUAL ANALYSIS

CHAPTER 7: THE QUESTION OF SEX

POINT OF VIEW

The point of view from which the story is told is changed once again as we are introduced to a third first-person narrator, this time a woman and a former Investigator, a member of the group of Investigators who had visited Gethen secretly two years earlier. She reports on the ambisexual physiology of the Gethenians and theorizes on their origin. Hers is the only voice of a woman in the book.

GENDER

In this chapter Le Guin explores the consequence of her own invention: the manwoman. This ambisexual condition completely equalizes man and woman: everyone can give birth, everyone is potentially a mother and a father. It abolishes the Oedipus complex, in which, according to Freud, every child experiences a psycho-sexual attraction to the parent of the opposite sex. It also abolishes all rape. Because the sexual drive is active only for a few days each month, life and relationship on Gethen are not governed by sexual drive as they are on Earth. Most of the time people are neutral, asexual, and sexuality is not a ruling social, economical, or political factor. All people are biologically the same and therefore all are equal.

WAR AND SEX

Le Guin postulates that the origin of wars is male aggression. There is no war on planet Gethen. Is it because the isolated male sexual activity is limited to a few days each month? War is "a vast Rape," says Le Guin, and by eliminating "the masculine that rapes and the femininity that is raped," war is abolished.

SENSE OF THE ABSURD

Speaking about people who are men-women, Le Guin delights in the absurd possibilities this idea offers her: "the mother of several children may be the father of several more." What is completely absurd on Earth is the norm on Gethen.

IRONY

The woman reporter writes that on Winter a person is judged and respected not as a man or a woman but as a human being - an ideal situation from a feminist point of view. Yet, this woman reporter finds the fact that she is not appreciated on Gethen as a woman "an appalling experience."

STYLE

This report by a woman Investigator is written in a different style than the rest of the book. It is very dry, matter-of-fact, resembling a textbook. This creates a break in the fictional narrative. The question that the reader may ask is whether this is the only way, or the best way, to introduce the Gethenians' unique sexual physiology. It is telling, not showing. We know but we do not see or feel. Nowhere in this chapter or in any other part of the book does Le Guin actually show how two Gethenians relate to each other intimately, or how they relate to their children in a family or hearth situation.

THE LEFT HAND OF DARKNESS

TEXTUAL ANALYSIS

CHAPTER 8: ANOTHER WAY INTO ORGOREYN

POINT OF VIEW

Once again we have Ai's first-person narration. As he tells of his journey around the country of Karhide and his entry into Orgoreyn, we see the country through his eyes.

EDUCATION OF THE ENVOY

This is an important step in Ai's education. Failing in his mission with the king of Karhide, Ai, in a way, is forced to roam the country and learn the ways of its people. Although he is unaware of it, his close contact with the people themselves, and his own experiences of their harsh life in a world of ice, is imperative for the completion of his mission. Not high-level politics but direct contact with and understanding of the people themselves will help him bring about Gethen's entrance into the League of the Planets.

AIMS DOES NOT JUSTIFY MEANS

Does the aim of the public good justify the sacrifice, or even the suffering, of an individual? The different answers to this philosophical and ethical question have been the crux of important political theories of the right and of the left. Le Guin gives her answer very clearly: the aim, however grand, does not justify the means. A mission that "overrides all personal debts and loyalties ... is an immoral mission."

Ai, at this stage of his life, thinks differently. His mission, he states, is more important than personal debt and loyalties. He refuses to carry money to Estraven, now considered a traitor, because it will endanger his mission, even though he is well aware that Estraven has been exiled for supporting him. Is this an act of betrayal? of cowardice? Luckily, Ai realizes in time that he is about to commit a moral error and betray not only Estraven but the Ekumen itself, whose principle is that the aim does not justify the means. With courage, Ai admits his mistake and shortcoming and agrees to deliver the money.

CHARACTERIZATION: AI

Ai has not learned all his lessons yet. When he crosses the border to Orgoreyn, and meets what seems like law and order, in complete opposition to the anarchy and chaos of Karhide, he misjudges the new country the same way he has misjudged Karhide. He is impressed by external reality and is unable to interpret it. And so while driving across Orgoreyn, and later, when treated to comfort and luxury, he feels that this orderly country is ready to accept his mission and that he has wasted two years in Karhide. He could not have made a greater mistake. His misjudgment may cost him his life.

THE LEFT HAND OF DARKNESS

TEXTUAL ANALYSIS

CHAPTER 10: CONVERSATIONS IN MISHNORY

POINT OF VIEW

Continuation of Ai's first-person narration. He tells of his meeting with Estraven and then with the rulers of Orgoreyn, and reports accurately, in detail, all the conversations they carry on. This method of direct speech (reporting in quotation marks the exact words of the speaker) allows us to see the situation and the people not only from Ai's limited point of view but also from their own words.

However, because this chapter presents a number of characters who play the same or similar roles, Ai's limited point of view, especially because he himself is unfamiliar with these characters, presents a real obstacle to the clarity of the story. Here is one place where we wish the writer would explain things more.

CHARACTERIZATION: AI

Impressed by the luxury his host lavishes on him, and assuming that the Orgota rulers are interested in his mission, Ai, feeling some sense of power, reveals a dark and unpleasant side of his character. When Estraven was a powerful Prime Minister, Ai showed him respect and sought his help. Now that Estraven has lost his power, his position and his country, and cannot be of any further help, or so Ai assumes, he treats him arrogantly, humiliates him, and refers to him derogatorily as "that fellow." Although his conscience "itched a little," he feels that he and Estraven will never develop a "tolerable relationship." The unfortunate result is that he fails to heed Estraven's warning.

Ai is blind to what is really happening around him, just as he is blind to the decisive role Estraven is playing. Only slowly does he begin to sense that his Orgota hosts are not truly interested in his mission and that each faction is trying to use him for a purpose of its own. He is duly alarmed.

IRONY

Ai admits that an integral part of his job is "high-flown speculation" called Farfetching, which can be explained as intuitive understanding, an extremely important quality when one finds himself in new situations. Although Ai was trained for this, he frankly divulges that he was never especially good at it. As proof, throughout his sojourn on Gethen, he consistently fails to understand, or "farfetch," the people and events around him. Here in Orgoreyn, it requires the help of Estraven to show him that things are not as they seem to be and that truth has evaded him.

CHARACTERIZATION: SHUSGIS, OBSLE, SLOSE, YEGEY

These Orgota members of the Commensality are flat characters, lacking in substance and in personality. They are functional characters; that is, they are in the story to advance the plot and to deliver certain information, but they have no life of their own as characters, as people. Consequently, it is difficult for us to distinguish them one from the other.

This may well be Le Guin's intention: Toward the end of the chapter, Ai stresses his feeling that the people in Orgoreyn are vague and lack in substance. They may be so, but as characters they are interchangeable and blur into each other. Because Ai himself does not know what these people really think and what their real intention is, we, being solely dependent on his observation, get lost. In addition, their weird and hard-to-pronounce names further confound the readers.

THEME: CASTING NO SHADOWS

Ai is right when he feels that in Orgoreyn people "did not cast shadows." Only ghosts do not cast shadows. And ghostlike, the people around him are "unreal," "vague," "blurred," "not solid" and lacking "some dimension of being." The buildings, too, are blurred, insubstantial, their corners vague-a city of monoliths. Only later, when it is too late, does Ai learn the truth, that in Orgoreyn appearance is completely different from reality. In fact, the country is run by secret police, having an elaborate network of prisons and labor camps.

In contrast, Estraven appears "shadowlike." There are no dark secrets or lies or pretense in Estraven. He has, as Ai described in his first report (Chapter 1), "a solidness of being, a substantiality." But Ai is taken in by the lies of Orgoreyn and so mistrusts the honesty of Estraven.

Ai comments that Orgoreyn calls "the part and the whole by the same name." Here Le Guin clearly refers to the Tao and its concept of the whole as the sum of two opposites, good and evil, light and darkness. However, Orgoreyn does not acknowledge its own "shadowy" aspect, pretending only a light side and declaring that to be the whole. Because Orgoreyn denies half of its existence, the entire country and its people seem unreal, vague, and lacking in substance.

SCIENCE FICTION

Le Guin elaborates on the way her Envoy from Earth has arrived on planet Gethen and the way he expects to leave it. A star ship manned with eleven other members brought Ai to Gethen's solar system, from where he took a space ship to land on Gethen. Now the star ship is orbiting around the Gethenian sun with the eleven crew members in a state of hibernation, waiting for Ai's message to wake them up. When the message arrives, they will be able to land on Gethen in a matter of days.

STRUCTURE AND STYLE

A great part of the chapter consists of the questioning of Ai by the Orgota rulers followed by his often long and explanatory answers.

More than in any other chapter, Ai's **diction** is steeped in Earth lingo, such as "that fellow"; "My conscience itched a little"; "the man was like an electric shock." This is especially so when he recounts his feelings toward Estraven. He sounds coarse, even rude. In contract, Estraven, even when he is humiliated and upset, as we will learn later, uses a very elegant, even musical speech inclined toward the poetic: "There they said you were; here they'll say you're not ..." or, "Banished men should never speak their native tongue; it comes bitter from their mouth."

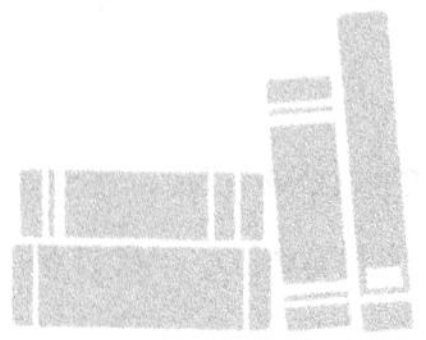

THE LEFT HAND OF DARKNESS

TEXTUAL ANALYSIS

CHAPTER 11: SOLILOQUIES IN MISHNORY

POINT OF VIEW AND STRUCTURE

Estraven's first-person narration. This consists of entries in his diary, and therefore the writing is fragmentary, reflecting the movement of the mind more than the sequence of events.

This chapter overlaps the time period of the former chapter, and in an interesting way serves as a distorted mirror: we go through some of the same events, some of the same conversations, but from another person's point of view, and so we perceive a different picture.

Because Estraven, an experienced politician, is familiar with the inside politics of Orgoreyn, his analysis of the situation and of the rulers of Orgoreyn provides us with a necessary clarification of the situation.

CHARACTERIZATION: ESTRAVEN

Estraven is fully committed to his own mission: bringing peace and harmony to the planet Gethen, which is currently threatened by the evil doings of Tibe of Karhide and the rulers of Orgoreyn. Also, as a true statesman, he knows that the way to change a situation is not by opposing it but by offering an alternative. Alliance with the Ekumen, the League of the Planets, is such an alternative, and so at great personal risk, he dedicates his life to the larger goal, sacrificing personal status, power, and homeland.

POLITICAL SITUATION

Analyzing the complex political situation in Orgoreyn, Estraven recounts the efforts carried by one small faction of the Orgota Commensals, the Open Traders, led by Yegey, to win over a majority in the government by using the Envoy and his sensational space ship. However, the rulers of the secret police, the Sarf, who are in the majority, oppose the Envoy and any change that the completion of his mission would necessarily bring to the country. In addition, the uncommitted members of the commensal fear that the Envoy and his space ship are a hoax invented by Karhide.

Estraven's clear analysis helps us understand that Orgoreyn is a very repressive police state. The secret police control all communication. They control what people know and thus what people think. Thus, no word about the Envoy has been heard on the radio. The public in Orgoreyn is not aware of the existence of the Envoy. Estraven knows that silence is ominous and threatens the Envoy's life.

CHARACTERIZATION: AI

By having both her **protagonists** tell their stories in first-person narration, Le Guin provides us with the objectivity necessary to see each of them from both the inside and the outside. Through Estraven's account of Ai, we can see Ai in a way that his own narrative cannot provide.

Estraven notes that Ai has improved his skill as an Envoy since he left Karhide. He has become more experienced. Estraven appreciates Ai's well-made speech; however, he still finds him largely inexperienced, innocent, and impatient.

Ai's speech to the thirty-three Members of the Commensal is met with persistent incredulity by the dominant faction, who are sure that he is a Karhidish agent. They demand more proof of Ai's authenticity, and this he cannot provide.

Estraven, alarmed by the turn of events and fearing for Ai's life, warns him that he is in danger and advises him to bring down his star ship.

GENDER

Le Guin offers us a rare glimpse of an ambisexual Gethenian in kemmer, meaning in sexual heat. However, as on Earth, the intensity of the sexual drive can be manipulated into sexual intrigue as demonstrated by Gaum, a high official in the Secret Police. He is certain that Estraven's plan is to bring loss of prestige to Orgoreyn by promoting the Envoy's hoax. Through hormone-induced "kemmer" and sexual advances, he tries to seduce Estraven to come with him to a government-run public kemmerhouse.

THE LEFT HAND OF DARKNESS

TEXTUAL ANALYSIS

CHAPTERS 12 AND 13

CHAPTER 12: ON TIME AND DARKNESS

This chapter tells of the religion of Orgoreyn, the Yomesh cult. It belongs to the series of myths and legends of planet Gethen and serves as a counterpart to Chapter 5, which tells of the Handdara, the ancient religion of Karhide.

The Yomesh cult emerged from the Handdara two thousand years ago, when the impossible question, "What is the meaning of life?" was forced on the Foretellers. Their leader, the Weaver Meshe, then experienced permanent enlightenment and was able to see past and future not only for one moment but for the rest of his life. It was Meshe who created the new religion of Orgoreyn.

This explains why the central belief of the Yomesh cult is that eternal light is the force behind all things, and results in total exclusion of darkness, the negative side of life.

Although Le Guin does not openly criticize the Yomesh cult and does not try to prove it wrong, she suggests in this chapter that there is an unacknowledged dark side inherent in the Orgoreyn religion. But as darkness - acknowledged or not - does exist, it must be hidden. It becomes secretive and thus all the more evil- the **theme** of the following chapter.

The ending of this myth is revealing: "One center, one seeing, one law, one light," - oneness as opposed to duality. This is in sheer opposition to the Karhidish belief in plurality, where people "do not march in step" but exercise "many rhythms" (Chapter 1).

CHAPTER 13: DOWN ON THE FARM

Chapter 13 illustrates what Le Guin has been preparing us for in the Orgota myth: the cult of oneness and eternal light has forced darkness to go underground; and there, in the underground, it is a perpetual nightmare.

POINT OF VIEW

Ai's first-person narration tells of his arrest and ordeal in a locked van that travels for days. He is beginning to put things together and to grasp his earlier misunderstanding of Orgoreyn. The appearance of law and order that he admired, so different from the chaotic Karhide, is only a misleading cover to what is really going on underneath. All the apparent glitter is a hoax and a sham. Unfortunately, his awakening to the truth is too late to save him.

LIGHT IN THE DARKNESS

True to her belief that light and darkness always go hand in hand, Le Guin offers some light in the midst of the nightmare: human kindness, the only thing that naked and exposed people still have. So, in the bitter cold, somehow, the three most vulnerable persons, Ai and two others, always find themselves in the warmest place, protected in the middle of the huddle of bodies.

IN STEP

A recurrent **theme**: People who believe in oneness and reject duality lose their individuality and become subservient to a stronger, and usually evil, power. The group of Orgota prisoners thrown together in the truck resembles a passive headless body. Trained to discipline and submission, the group has no spokesman and no leader and no individual initiative. There is no talk, no communication, only deep silence.

GENDER

The only person trying to communicate with Ai and touch his hand is someone in kemmer. When Ai realizes that the person in heat is temporarily a female, he regrets that "the one time any one of them asked anything of me, ... I couldn't give it." Why? Le Guin does not clarify. Does she suggest here that mating with a Gethenian is biologically impossible? Or, that Ai is so steeped in his Earth **conventions** that even in an extreme situation he cannot accept the feminine aspects of man?

One thing is puzzling: Throughout the book, not even once does a Gethenian in kemmer turn male. The only example of a male in kemmer seems to be Ai himself, whose male sexual identity is constantly dominant, while the Gethenians' female sexual identity is dominant only four days every month.

In the labor camp, Ai feels for the first time on Winter that he is a man among women, or rather "among eunuchs," meaning lacking in maleness. During his stay on Winter, Ai, conditioned to regard people as either men or women and unable to accept a person who is both, looks at the Gethenians primarily as men. So what makes him feel now that he is among women? No positive things: it is their "flabbiness and coarseness." their "gross, bland fleshiness, a bovinity without point or edge," and their trivial talk.

IRONY

Le Guin is ironic when she points out that here, on Earth, and mainly by males, it is considered natural and desirable to be in "kemmer," sexual heat, all the time. However, it is the inmates in the labor camp who jeer at Ai for being constantly "in kemmer," and nickname him "the Pervert." This is not new to Ai for he has been called "the Pervert" by other Gethenians. The irony becomes even stronger when Ai is asked whether to be "in kemmer" all the time, meaning to be controlled by one's sexuality, is a reward or punishment. To his credit he admits that he does not know the answer. This may be the first doubt that he has expressed concerning the rightness of his sexuality and it may signify the beginning of his understanding and even acceptance of the Gethenians' ambisexuality.

Drugs are administered to the prisoners to control their sexuality and suppress the "kemmer" phase, creating "chemical castration." The result is sexless people, without shame and desire. And Le Guin rightly comments, though Ai, that it is not human to be without shame and desire.

NARRATIVE STYLE

In this chapter, the narrative takes a new turn and develops in a linear way, resembling more the structure of an adventure story, clear and absorbing and skillfully written.

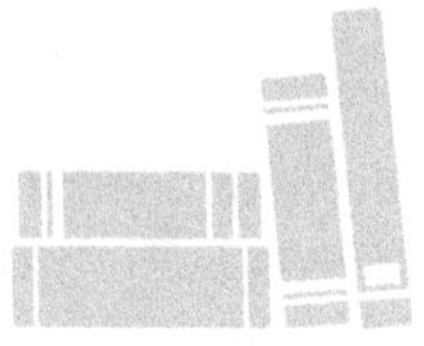

THE LEFT HAND OF DARKNESS

TEXTUAL ANALYSIS

CHAPTER 14: THE ESCAPE

....

POINT OF VIEW

Estraven, in first-person narration, tells in detail of his preparations to rescue Ai from the notorious labor camp.

ESTRAVEN AND AI

This is the beginning of the long and gradual alliance between Estraven and Ai. It is the first time they talk with each other person-to-person and not in their formal political roles. This is also the first time they find themselves outside organized society, alone in the vast, sparsely populated, snow-covered Hinterlands, huddled together inside a tiny tent half buried in the snow.

This forced intimacy provides their first real chance to develop mutual understanding and acceptance, and these will form the basis for the interplanetary alliance. Estraven, the more visionary and insightful person to the two, has long understand this and has offered Ai his full trust. However, the young, inexperienced, and immature Ai has rejected Estraven and as a result has had to go through many experiences in order to learn, mature, and reach the level of expanded humanity necessary to accept and trust the "Other."

As Estraven is explaining to Ai what had really happened in Karhide, once again we realize how much of the trouble Ai went through was due to his lack of insight into events and people. "All this I thought you understood, and in that I erred," Estraven complains. Likewise, Ai was completely ignorant of Estraven's active role in all that happened in Orgoreyn, including Ai's permit to enter the country. It seems that only now does Ai confront the real story of the events of which he had so little understanding and in which Estraven had played such a decisive role.

Ai rightly complains that Estraven should have given him all this information earlier and saved both of them from the dangerous labor camp. Even now he does not admit that he was not ready to listen and trust Estraven even if the latter had confided in him. Ai had held himself aloof from the Gethenians and thought he could offer them alliance on a political level while ignoring the essential personal alliance.

Even now, after listening to Estraven, after having been rescued by him from certain death, Ai is still mistrustful and wonders how he can believe what Estraven is telling him. Estraven is deeply hurt, "I am the only man in all Gethen that has trusted you entirely, and I am the only man in Gethen that you have refused to trust." Then he asks Ai to teach him mindspeech, the language that does not lie, to prove that he does not lie and can be trusted.

SCIENCE FICTION

In his dangerous rescue of Ai from the labor camp, Estraven uses self-induced do the-strength, an increased strength and energy a person can experience for a short period when in great need or in crisis, somewhat like the adrenaline-induced activity we experience in times of stress.

STYLE AND READER-INVOLVEMENT

When writing on personal relationships, Le Guin is at her best, engaging not only our intellect and admiration for her innovative ideas, but also our emotions. We become personally involved in these characters and watch them emerge as full-blooded people, no longer just the role-players or agents of their writer-inventor.

THE LEFT HAND OF DARKNESS

TEXTUAL ANALYSIS

CHAPTER 15: TO THE ICE

POINT OF VIEW

Ai's first-person narration is almost exclusively an observation of Estraven. For once Ai speaks not only as "I" but also as "Eye." Ai's narration overlaps the last part of Estraven's in the previous chapter. This allows us a partial double view of characters and events.

CHARACTERIZATION: AI

Ai finds himself alone with a person he mistrusts, far away from any populated area, in a province outside established norms, no longer restrained by habits and social expectations. In this wilderness of snow, stripped of his role as an Envoy, just as Estraven is stripped of his political role, there are only himself and Estraven, two equally vulnerable human beings, aliens in a hostile environment, battling the elements to survive.

Ai's progress into maturity is evident in the way he is finally able to relate to Estraven as person to person. It is the first time he genuinely observes Estraven as a human being and not as a tool to be used in his mission. Seeing him in his sleep, sweating and defenseless, Ai is finally able to see Estraven as he actually is, not the "Other," but a human being like himself.

Ai is learning to sense beneath the surface of Estraven's words. What had caused his mistrust in the first place was what Ai perceived as Estraven's irony-saying one thing and meaning something else. Now Ai understands that Estraven speaks with "complete simplicity" and that he, Ai, had mistaken honesty for irony.

Observing Estraven as a person, Ai is able to appreciate, even admire, Estraven's extraordinary qualities such as his ability to adjust to change, a remarkable quality if we consider how most people tend to resist change. Moreover, Ai is able to reach the interesting conclusion that this extraordinary quality has been the benchmark of Estraven's political career, as well as what has made him the only person on Gethen to believe in the Envoy and understand the real significance of Ai's mission. For that, Estraven has sacrificed his career and his homeland.

Ai, in the process of increasing his self-awareness, is able to look back and admit his folly, such as the way he humiliated Estraven when he loftily gave him the money sent from Ashe in Karhide. Ai understands that this is the very money Estraven has been using for Ai's rescue.

Ai finally realizes that had he heeded Estraven's warning and suggestion to call down his star ship, they would not be now in this life-threatening situation.

CHARACTERIZATION: ESTRAVEN

From the very first chapter Le Guin portrays Estraven as having "human grandeur." And true enough, he does display this quality in the courageous way he plans and executes Ai's rescue. However, the means he chooses to carry out his plan would be considered crimes by any legal system: forging documents, assuming a false name, lying, and worst of all, stealing (a terrible crime in Winter). Yet Estraven is capable of committing terrible crimes if they fit his goal.

This roundness and complexity of character fits well with Le Guin's theories of the coexistence of opposites, of light and darkness, good and evil, all necessary for wholeness.

Estraven's complexity of character also serves Le Guin's predilection toward the relativity of life: crime in one context is a heroic act in another.

THEME OF PATRIOTISM

Once again Le Guin explores the concept of patriotism and shows its absurdity. It is always Ai who speaks of love or hate for one's country, and it is always Estraven who questions it. Estraven declares his love for the land he knows, but does not understand how a border, an artificial division, can put an end or a limit to one's love for the land: "that sort of love does not have a boundary-line of hate."

GENDER

Now that Ai is in the process of changing his attitude toward Estraven and accepting him as he is, the question of gender takes on special significance. After all, Estraven, as he really is, is man and woman in one, something Ai has found almost impossible to comprehend. He has stubbornly continued to see all Gethenians as men, and their feminine traits have repelled him.

Huddled in the warmth of the tent, before they go to sleep, Ai and Estraven agree to address each other by their family names. On Gethen first names signify, as Estraven explains, "Hearth-brothers, or friends." This on Gethen is not as simple as it may be on Earth. Ai contemplates that on Gethen Hearth-brothers or friends may become lovers during their kemmering phase. This thought stirs deep conflicts in Ai, and in a very strong language he (admitting that he is locked into his virility) proclaims to himself that in this case he will not be friend to Estraven or to any one of his race. They were "no flesh of mine, no friend; no love between us," he declares. How has he ever thought of completing his mission and forging a friendly alliance between the planets if on a personal level he feels so strongly that he and the Gethenians are, and will ever be, aliens?

Le Guin finds Ai, the Earth male, sex-proud in another instance as well. When Ai is sick, he resents Estraven telling him to lie down and rest. He resents what he feels to be Estraven's patronizing, especially because Estraven is shorter than he is and "built more like a woman than a man, more fat than muscle." When they haul the sledge together, Ai, the taller and stronger of the two, feels like "a stallion in harness with a mule - "; he, Ai, strong and virile like a stallion, is side by side with a neuter. However, facing Estraven's frankness and simplicity, Ai has to confront his own flaw, his competitive manly pride, and admit to himself that Estraven has an advantage because he has "no standards of manliness, of virility, to complicate his pride."

While discussing love of one's country, Estraven proclaims his "ignorance," which, in Karhidish means he rejects abstraction. Ai's reaction is interesting; he sees the refusal to deal with the abstract as a feminine trait, and reacts with "displeasure." This echoes the passionate arguments between Feminists and male chauvinists of the 1960s and 1970s, with the latter often criticizing women as being unable to think in the abstract.

THEME OF BLOOD

After hunting, Estraven becomes the first Gethenian Ai sees "with blood on his hands." This connection between Estraven and blood is a recurrent **theme**. It takes us back to the first chapter, when Estraven explains to Ai that blood is the one real and lasting bonding in the mortar used to keep the keystone in the arch.

THEME OF THE JOURNEY

Since Homer's *Odyssey*, and even earlier, in the myths and legends of many people, the journey has served as a perennial symbol for life itself. In *The Left Hand of Darkness*, Le Guin offers us a journey within a journey within a journey. The first one is Ai's journey to the planet Gethen; the second is that of Ai and Estraven across 800 miles of wild desolation of snow and ice; and the third is Ai's inner journey into himself, and his growing self-awareness.

There, in a no-man's-land of snow and ice, both Estraven and Ai are so awed by the magnificent beauty of Glacier that they agree that it is the journey, more than its goal, that really matters. Many have said this before; but when said here by two people in terrible and imminent danger, in desolation and utter loneliness, out of all touch with human society, these words take on a greater meaning.

COEXISTENCE OF OPPOSITES

Even here, in the land of perennial snow and ice, Le Guin's landscape contains a wholeness made of opposites: "fiery mouths that opened out of the ice." And although the fire and the ice, the red and white landscape spell out death, Ai and Estraven, intoxicated with the breathtaking sight, laugh with joy.

SCIENCE FICTION

To make their journey in sub-zero temperatures possible, Le Guin invents for her travelers an ideal stove we could all use: a cook stove, heater, and lantern all in one, powered by a bionic battery and good for fourteen months' continuous use.

FANTASY

Le Guin is inventive when she creates for Gethen, a planet all her own, new vegetation and unheard-of animals: a poetic forest of "dwarfs, thick-set, gnarl-limbed, ice-bearded thore-trees." And the "pesthry," one of the larger land-animals of Winter, is the size of a fox, having splendid fur and edible meat.

STYLE

In this chapter the narrative picks up speed. Like the two travelers, the words seem to surge forward powerfully, accumulating energy and grandeur. The descriptions of invented landscapes of unusual grandeur expressed in minute detail and very precise language attest to Le Guin's complete control over her language and material. Here, story and words, content and form are skillfully integrated.

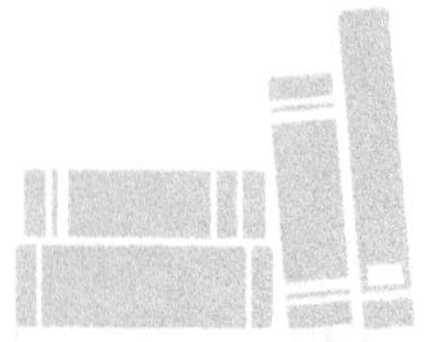

THE LEFT HAND OF DARKNESS

TEXTUAL ANALYSIS

CHAPTER 16: BETWEEN DRUMNER AND DREMEGOLE

POINT OF VIEW

Estraven's first-person narration. This chapter, too, relates the development of the intimate relationship between the two aliens, Ai and Estraven. While Estraven is watching and comparing Ai to himself, we get a chance to have a third-person view of Ai, whom we know mainly through his own words. As both **protagonists** learn "to pull together," the narrator's voice becomes first-person plural; "I" becomes "we."

ESTRAVEN AND AI

Like Ai, Estraven has to learn to accept the entire personality of the person who is an alien to him. Although from the beginning Estraven accepted Ai, this is the first time that he lives with him, in close proximity. It is revealing when Estraven observes that Ai, who suffers greatly from the cold weather on Winter, sometimes "sweats like one of us" (in the previous chapter it is Ai who notices Estraven sweat and feels an affinity with him). Estraven acknowledges that this alien from outer space is flesh and blood, "like one of us," not just for philosophical or humanistic considerations, but on the gut level.

For both it is a continuous process of learning and adjusting. Although they sweat the same way, adjusting their heater to the cold temperatures is a problem, because "either's comfort is the other's pneumonia." But with a genuine effort to accept the other, they "strike a medium."

Both realize that they have much in common. Just as Estraven had to give up his powerful position and the right to live in his country for Ai and his mission, so Ai had to give up the world he knew, his family and friends (because he had timejumped, all the people he had known on Earth are dead by now) for the sake of Estraven and his planet; as Ai said, "You for my sake-I for yours."

Here, on the ice, far away from any human community, each of them is unique in his "Otherness" as well as in his aloneness, without a community of people to support his existence. That was the way Ai had lived for two years in Gethen, completely alone, without any support from his own people, while at the same time Estraven has had the entire population of Gethen to identify with. But now, on the ice, estranged from his fellow men, he too is one-of-a-kind, one and alone. Now, they are equal. The only thing that counts now is the one-to-one relationship.

The relationship between the two is tested when Estraven enters kemmer, and his physical awareness is at its peak. He is trying to avoid Ai, and when pressed by Ai, he explains his sensitive situation. Ai, instead of laughing as Estraven has expected him to, addresses him with gentleness. To his surprise, Estraven discovers that Ai possesses feminine qualities which he had not recognized before.

CHARACTERIZATION: ESTRAVEN

Estraven is able to see Ai's strengths and also to sympathize with his vulnerability. He does not criticize him even when he has grounds to but accepts him with generosity and empathy. Although Ai is physically stronger than Estraven and can haul heavier weight, his spirit is not as enduring and he is prey to despair. Once again Le Guin plays on the relativity of concepts: if Ai were a Gethenian, Estraven would have called him a coward. But accepting his "Otherness," he knows that Ai is no coward but actually brave and is ready to take risks.

Estraven discloses a surprising fact: when he had first heard about the Alien in Karhide, he asked for his name. When told the name was "Ai," he heard it as "a cry of pain from a human throat across the night." This new factor reveals that Estraven, the Prime Minister, has helped Ai not only for political reasons but from the very first as a human being helping another.

This disclosure leaves some open questions concerning Estraven in his public role as prime minister. Luckily, his helping Ai coincides with what is also good and beneficial for the planet in general. But were it not, would he have sacrificed the good of the nation to help the Envoy? In a way Le Guin has answered it by stressing throughout the book that the individual cannot be sacrificed for the common good.

GENDER

"What is a woman?" Le Guin asks through Estraven. Le Guin said that she had set out to write this novel with the purpose of discovering for herself what a woman is. Now, three quarters into the book, Estraven finally feels intimate enough with Ai to ask him what a woman is and whether she is different from a man.

Ai has no clear answer. "No. Yes. No," he falters. Then, struggling with words, he reveals that Earth society sets different expectations concerning women and men. When Estraven asks whether women are mentally inferior, Ai admits that he does not know, and still struggling to answer Estraven's question he finally admits defeat: he does not know what women are like. He concedes that women are alien to him even more so than Estraven is, because with Estraven he shares at least one sex. Ai's words underline what many of Le Guin's critics have complained about: that the Gethenians are men with something added, and woman is the stranger to both Ai and Estraven.

Ai's unanswer, to use Le Guin's language, reminds us of those questions that the Foretellers consider impossible to answer and that therefore should not be asked.

Le Guin points out that what men in our society regard as the symbol of their virility, their sexual organ, is visible and measurable in contrast to women's organ, which is inner and hidden. In fact, while women's lack of a penis prompted Freud to develop his prominent theory of penis envy, Le Guin, ironically, turns this theory upside down. It is Estraven who pities Ai exactly for being so exposed "even to his sexual organ which he must carry always outside himself." And taking into consideration the extreme cold weather on Gethen, this can be a real hardship.

Le Guin is also ironic when she describes Ai as being always conscious of his manhood. When he tries hard not to cry and fails, he hides his face and Estraven cannot understand this curious behavior. Estraven, after all, is a manwoman, ignorant of the male's false pride in his virility on Earth.

LEFT HAND OF DARKNESS

Estraven quotes a Karhidish poem, which provides the title to the book and signifies its main idea: light and darkness are both two sides of the same thing, both are one. This, as we have already observed, is the Taoist holistic view of life, a wholeness composed of opposites. Ai himself observes that the Handdara, Karhide's religion, is less interested in the gap between humans and animals, as Earth people are, but are more interested in "the likeness, the links, the whole of which living things are a part."

The poem has clear references to one of the main scenes of the book. In the love story between Estraven's ancestors, the Lord of Estre and the Lord of Stok (Chapter 9), who were lovers in kemmer, they find that their hands, when touching one another, match exactly. Now, it is Estraven and Ai who share intimacy, and although they prefer not to touch one another and not to communicate sexually, they are nevertheless on the point of communicating in "mindspeech," the highest or most intimate form of communication between people.

TIMEJUMPING

Le Guin, like many other science fiction writers, is fascinated by the manifold possibilities created by moving as fast as light, suggesting that one does not age while travelling at that speed. This creates the absurd possibility that Ai, who is not yet thirty years old, was actually born 125 years ago. Thus, he timejumped about 95 years during the five years he spent in the star ship, while at the same time many years had passed on Earth; his parents died (seventy years ago) and so did all the people he had known on Earth.

This proves that he had to sacrifice a great deal for the mission he undertook voluntarily to bring the Gethenians into an alliance with the League of the Planets. However, Le Guin does not deal with Ai's return to Earth: If he must timejump those same 95 years, he would be only about a decade older than when he left, and he would find all the people he knew still alive.

STRUCTURE

This is a central chapter in the book. It seems as if the entire narrative-Ai's journey to planet Gethen, as well as Estraven and Ai's risky journey across the ice-leads to the scene in which Ai and Estraven are completely alone and dependent on each other and have to deal with their differences and likenesses, to come to terms with the wholeness of their relationship. Likewise, it is the first chapter in which the first person narrative is actually double, Estraven's and Ai's alternately. What has been a strictly singular voice before becomes a double voice, a duet.

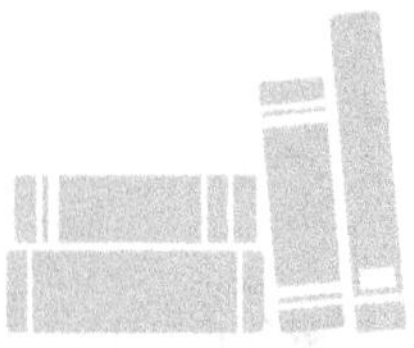

THE LEFT HAND OF DARKNESS

TEXTUAL ANALYSIS

CHAPTER 17: AN ORGOTA CREATION MYTH

STRUCTURE

This is the last of the myths and legends of the planet Gethen. If the first half of the book offers myths and legends of Karhide, the second half offers the same of Orgoreyn, the other country on the planet.

This chapter is linked to the other Orgota myth (Chapter 12) "On Time and Darkness." But whereas the earlier legend centers on eternal light, this one centers on the threat of darkness to swallow the world. In each case, it is either light or darkness, one threatening the other. Le Guin makes the Orgota myths a counterpart to those of Karhide which offer wholeness as the view of life. Although she does not offer any value judgment, her preferences are implied.

THE MYTH

The Orgota myth of creation begins with the sun and ice, all light and whiteness and no shadows. The melting of the ice creates the world, beasts, and people. The people, thirty-nine brothers, through betrayal and death, introduce darkness into the world of light.

FRATERNAL BETRAYAL

This is another version of the recurrent **theme** of brothers' incestuous relationships which result in offspring. In this Orgota creation myth, one brother, caught by inexplicable fear, kills thirty-seven of his brothers and mates with the last surviving one, giving birth to "the nations of men."

Each of the offspring is followed by "a piece of darkness," a shadow, which will eventually "eat the light," and nothing will be left in the world but ice and darkness. Le Guin's message is clear: where there is no balance and coexistence, there is death and destruction.

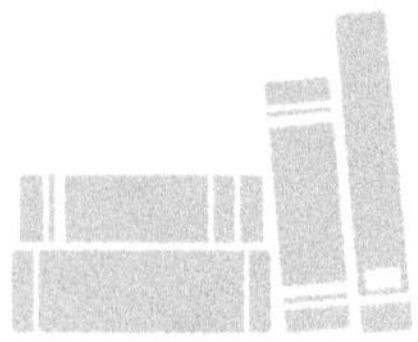

THE LEFT HAND OF DARKNESS

TEXTUAL ANALYSIS

CHAPTER 18: ON THE ICE

POINT OF VIEW

This chapter mirrors Chapter 16 and recounts many of the same events and conversations but from Ai's point of view. However, this is a somewhat different Ai, more mature, more contemplative.

STRUCTURE

Far from being repetitive, this skillful double-telling becomes a powerful technique that intensifies our emotions and increases our suspense. Knowing what one of the pair in a relationship thinks and feels, we are terribly curious to know what the other feels about the same events. By making it possible, Le Guin lets us feel as if we have gone through Alice's looking glass.

GENDER

For the first time Ai is able to discuss the Gethenian sexuality with understanding, not with disgust, a proof of the degree of maturity he has reached. This signifies the **climax** of their relationship as Ai is finally able to accept the feminine aspect of Estraven, accept that Estraven is both a man and a woman.

Ai is able to acknowledge the sexual tension between them, which is "admitted and understood." His acceptance and trust make space for real and profound friendship, called "now as later, love." This may be the most profound form of love because it is based not on what the lovers have in common, but on their differences.

In his report Ai finds it necessary to explain why the two of them have not consummated their love sexually: the sexual act would only have accentuated how alien they were to each other. Theirs is a touch of souls as profound as it can be. Yet Ai himself has doubts. He is not sure that his explanation is right, and in courageously admitting this, he attests not only to his honesty but also to his aroused sexuality. He has never before felt this attraction toward any of the Gethenians, not even when he was approached by one in a female phase when they were naked in the truck on the way to the work farm.

Some critics regard Le Guin's apparent refusal to describe a scene of physical lovemaking between Ai and Estraven as a failure, a weakness or a lack of daring. This may be so. It is possible that she did not have the courage to take her **protagonists** all the way. However, it could instead reflect Le Guin's need to refute Freud, saying that profound love between individuals does not have to be based on sex.

NONVERBAL COMMUNICATION

Now that Ai acknowledges his love for Estraven, he offers him the only thing he can offer a Gethenian: mindspeech, the most profound and intimate method of communication.

When they finally manage to mindspeak, Estraven is overwhelmed because what he hears emerge from the depth of his soul is not Ai's voice but his dead brother's voice, and he calls out, "Arek! Is that you?" This is a clear reference to the first Karhidish legend, "The Place Inside the Blizzard" (Chapter 2), the ancient tale of the love and betrayal of two brothers. This is the first time that Estraven clearly associates Ai with his own dead brother.

But this scene also refers to Estraven's admitting that the name "Ai" reminded him of a cry of pain, which he could not ignore and which touched his deepest feelings. Although in Ai's name Estraven could have heard just as well "I" or "Eye," it is the cry of pain that he chose to hear, a nonverbal cry, a kind of mindspeech. Has he been touched so deeply because on first hearing this cry of pain he was reminded of the cry of his brother and lover, Arek? Is that why Estraven sacrificed name, position, power and country, and later his life, so that his lost lover might come to life again in the form of an Envoy from another planet?

I AND THOU: BUBER AND BARRETT

Ai and Estraven have now reached the acme of relationships, and Ai recognizes that they can no longer speak as "We and They; not I and It; but I and Thou."

For the first time Ai understands the deep meaning of his mission and the reason he was sent alone to the new planet: only alone can he develop an individual, personal relationship with another human being here. Only alone can he be changed by the alien world and learn to accept it and its people on the level of existence rather than just on the impersonal political level.

In his book *I and Thou,* the philosopher Martin Buber (1878–1965) expounded his most important theory of the relationship between I and Thou. When a person treats another as an object, his relationship becomes "I and It." The "I - It" relationship, in which the Other is viewed objectively and is judged and observed, is not a genuine relationship. However, in the "I - Thou" relationship, the "Thou" is more than one thing among others in the universe. The whole universe is seen in the light of the "Thou." Buber argues that the "I" of the "I - It" relationship is completely different from the "I" of the "I - Thou" pair, because the relationship itself transforms the "I."

Buber maintains that in the "I - It" relationship only a part of ourselves is involved and a part always remains outside, observing. But in the "I - Thou" relationship our whole being must be involved. If we keep any part to ourselves, even a small part, we stay as spectators and regress to the "I - It" relationship. The "I - Thou" relationship is risky, because our whole existence is involved. There is no defense left.

William Barrett, in *Irrational Man* (1958), explains that the "meaning in life happens in the area between person and person ... when one says I to the other's Thou." In this kind of relationship each person has to confront the other in completeness, with his whole being, with complete trust, opening up to the other while still retaining one's own identity.

It is not a confrontation of two rational minds searching for rational explanation but a meeting "on the level of existence."

When Ai (I?) says to Estraven "I and Thou," he has progressed a long way. Earlier in Karhide, when asked by Ashe, Estraven's former lover (Chapter 8), to deliver money to Estraven the Traitor, Ai replies that his mission "overrides all personal debts and loyalties." Now, on the Gobrin Ice, he realizes that the Ekumen is a mystical rather than a political body, and its doctrine is just the reverse of what he had told Ashe. Now he knows that the end does not justify the means, that his mission is a process of personal relationship, not a political event.

Now that Ai and Estraven have reached the apex of human relationships, the state of I and Thou, they are ready to enter the place inside the blizzard.

THEME OF TWO BROTHERS

Ai and Estraven reach the place inside the blizzard where it is all white and windless and shadowless, a place we remember from the legend of "The Place Inside the Blizzard" (Chapter 2). Now everything falls into place, because in the place inside the blizzard live all those who kill themselves, and here, according to the old Karhide myth, lives Hode, who had committed suicide rather than break his vow with his brother. And it is in the place inside the blizzard, according to the old legend, that the two brothers, the living and the dead, meet again.

In the old legend, the dead brother, having broken his vow by his suicide, cannot call the living brother by his name. Estraven, hearing Ai call him in mindspeech by his first name, Therem, calls out excitedly, "You can call me by my name!" For Estraven, the dead brother has been resurrected in Ai.

Although Le Guin only suggests here the story of Estraven and his brother, we have received in earlier chapters enough clues to construct a story similar to the old Karhide myth of the two brothers who defied the code of incest by swearing eternal love to each other. Estraven himself tells Ai very little about his brother Arek who died fourteen years ago, and for whose sake apparently Estraven had left home, or was forced to leave, six years earlier. We also know that it was "the only true vow of faithfulness he has ever sworn" and that it was wordless, as is the mindspeech with which he can finally communicate with Ai.

As discussed earlier, Bruno Bettelheim tells us, in the *The Uses of Enchantment*, that the **theme** of the two brothers in fairy tales implies that complete attachment to the past and to the parental home can lead to disaster, and that one needs to learn to separate oneself from one's childhood and home, reaching toward the future and creating an independent life.

Now, Estraven, whose emotions have been completely tied up with his dead brother for many years, learns to relate to a new person, Ai, on the deep emotional level on which he previously had related to his brother. It is the first time that we see Estraven so emotionally overwhelmed and shaken, and it is the first time that he is ready to share with Ai something about his brother Arek. Ai learns that the light of truth that mindspeech brings can also illuminate the depth of the sorrow and darkness in the human soul.

THE LEFT HAND OF DARKNESS

TEXTUAL ANALYSIS

CHAPTER 19: HOMECOMING

POINT OF VIEW

This is a continuation of Ai's first-person narration but with a significant difference. Until now he has almost always begun his reports with his first person I featuring prominently in the very first sentence: "I'll make" (Chapter 1), "I slept" (Chapter 3), "I awoke" (Chapter 15), or "Next morning as I finished..." (Chapter 10), etc. (Only Chapter 5 begins differently: with "My landlady"). However, in this chapter the I is largely replaced by we. From the very beginning of this chapter the first-person plural, we, predominates and for a while it is impossible to know whose voice it is, Ai's or Estraven's.

SETTING

Le Guin creates a surrealistic landscape inside the blizzard, where everything is totally white, so white and bright in fact that it creates no shadows. And having no shadows means that it is almost impossible to detect any crevasse, cracks, or wrinkles in the land, or rather in the ice. This white landscape of "zero weather" is "the absence of everything," a "floor of nothing." Le Guin paints a powerful image, telling us that to be where all is white, all light, is also to be where there is absence, nothing, zero.

This setting serves well to visually illustrate Le Guin's prevalent theory that light without darkness is destructive, that only together can light and darkness maintain the balance necessary for survival.

CHARACTERIZATION: AI

In this landscape of whiteness with no shadows, where one cannot see his way, Ai is paralyzed with fear. However, for the first time in his life he actually admits being desperately afraid. This is a small step forward on the ice, but a giant one in the development of his self-awareness.

Now that Ai has accepted Estraven's femininity, he is beginning to be able to accept his own feminine aspects which previously he had considered to be identified exclusively with women: being vulnerable, weak, afraid. To Ai's credit we must say that he finds the courage to break the final barrier of his manly pride, to accept and even voice his vulnerability.

THEME OF SHADOW

Estraven teaches Ai that fear is useful and necessary and that far from being an exclusively female characteristic, it is essential to survival, as are darkness and shadows.

In her essay "The Child and the Shadow" (found in *The Language of the Night*, 1979) Le Guin explains that the shadow reflects the hidden and dark side of human nature, "the dark brother of the conscious mind," everything "we don't want to, can't admit into our conscious self, all the qualities ... within us which have been repressed, denied, or not used." She quotes Carl Jung: "Everyone carries a shadow, and the less it is embodied in the individual's conscious life, the blacker and denser it is." When a person faces reality, she explains, he "must admit that the hateful, the evil, exists within himself." One cannot blame others; one has to shoulder responsibility for his own problems and for the problems of our world.

She phrased this idea differently in her "A Left-Handed Commencement Address" (1983). Speaking to the graduates of Mills College, mainly women, about failure, she said, "What I hope for you ... is that you will be able to live there, in the dark place. To live in the place that our rationalizing culture of success denies, calling it a place of exile, uninhabitable, foreign."

Finally Ai understands. To prove it he draws the yin-yang symbol of the double curve within the circle, the Taoist symbol of the coexistence of opposites. When Estraven does not understand this symbol, Ai demonstrates his understanding of the Gethenians' mind by being able to translate his Earth views into Gethenians' understanding. He explains that the yin-yang symbol is the same idea as "light is the left hand of darkness" and as "Female, male. It is yourself, Therem. Both and one. A shadow on snow."

If we remember that in the first chapter Ai had confessed that after two years on Winter he was "still far away from being able to see the people of the planet through their own eyes," we can appreciate the giant step he has made. By being able to see Estraven through Estraven's eyes, Ai has learned to see through the eyes of the Gethenians as a whole. Moreover, Ai is able to relate the Gethenians' basic philosophy of life to an Earth philosophy, and find a common ground within their differences.

This completes Ai's total acceptance and understanding of Estraven as he is, accepting the differences and appreciating the similarities. Both Ai and Estraven, in full understanding and mutual acceptance, are ready to come home.

THE DARK AND THE BRIGHT

Although the last few days provide easy travel in hospitable land, they are also the hardest because both voyagers realize that separation awaits them at the end of the road. The joy that has accompanied their hardest days together turns to grief.

Even the landscape of this hospitable land reflects the light and the darkness of their souls: the sun is "cold in a bright sky," sending "shadows," and the road is "streaked with dark and bright."

CHARACTERIZATION: AI

Once again Ai demonstrates his new understanding and maturity. When he finally radios the message to his star ship he has no way to know if his message will be received. It is a matter of life or death, yet, instead of fretting anxiously, he accepts the uncertainty with a "quiet heart." He has clearly learned an important lesson from the Foretellers (Chapter 5): that the only thing we can be certain about is uncertainty. Ai has learned to accept life as life really is.

But he has one more lesson to learn: the price of profound love. Love gained and love lost go hand in hand, as joy and sorrow, light and darkness. As they reach their goal and the successful end of the journey, Ai loses what he has so painfully gained-love and intimacy with another person. After he has experienced the profundity of love he has to experience the profundity of sorrow, and emerge from both with greater knowledge.

THEMES OF LOVE AND BETRAYAL

Love cannot lead to eternal happiness; just as light is always accompanied by darkness, love is joined by betrayal. And betrayal, in this last stage of the journey, comes both from the outside and from within.

From the outside: Estraven is betrayed by Thessicher, the very person he has trusted his life to and whom he had helped obtain his farm. Afraid of losing this farm, this farmer preferred to betray Estraven to his enemy, Tibe.

From within: Estraven dashes forward - "he ran from me," says Ai - toward the border straight into the guns of the borderguards. They shouted warnings but, rushing toward the fence, he did not stop. Did he commit suicide? Was a second separation, this time from his new-found love, too difficult for Estraven? Did he feel that death was better than another exile and another separation? He who had "grandeur of soul" and was so strong and resilient throughout, succumbs to his weaker side, and commits what in Karhide is considered the greatest crime of all, suicide. Weakness and strength, light and shadow, male and female, all in one.

But there in the space between these two betrayals, they experience the deepest love: when Ai accompanies Estraven to the border, they have to spend the night in the open snow. Unlike on their long journey on the ice, this time they have neither tent nor stove. Completely exposed to the elements, they have nothing but their deep bond of companionship.

And later, when Estraven is dying, Ai holds him. Estraven answers Ai's love in mindspeech, identifying Ai with his dead brother, Arek, and in this way Estraven is finally able to reconcile his past and his present. Love is affirmed once again but this time as a source of immeasurable pain.

STYLE

The entire chapter, but mainly the landscape over which Ai and Estraven are skiing to the border, signals the events to come, the confrontation with darkness. It is "a sunlight sky, a white world, and we two strokes of shadows on it, fleeing." They both huddle "in the dark hollow under the dark trees, in the snow," among trees of "reddish boughs," close to the border whose guards are "dots along the pallid snow," and whose markings are "pole-tops painted red." Then Estraven, through "the shadows over the snow," skies "straight into the guns." The setting is colored white and black and tainted with red.

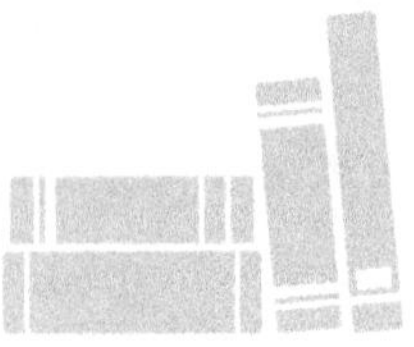

THE LEFT HAND OF DARKNESS

TEXTUAL ANALYSIS

CHAPTER 20: A FOOL'S ERRAND

POINT OF VIEW

This is Ai's first-person narration, summing up the story and his part in it. If we compare this last report to his first one (Chapter 1), we will find that the reports are written from two different points of view, although narrated by the same person. If the first report is narrated from the alien's point of view looking at the Gethenians as strangers, this last report is narrated from a Gethenian's point of view looking at the messengers from Earth as strangers and aliens.

CHARACTERIZATION: AI

Ai, who has learned from Estraven that there is no shame in being vulnerable, takes advantage of his new learning, and freely cries over the death of the person he has learned to love.

His sorrow is so deep that he finds no solace even in crying. This too he has yet to learn: to deal with the deepest sorrow.

The physician who takes care of him gives him Taoist advice in a beautiful **metaphor**, "Lie down like the rivers frozen in the valley in winter. Lie still. Wait." You cannot fight sorrow and it cannot be healed at will; it needs to be fully experienced.

THEME OF BETRAYAL

Finally, in his audience with the king of Karhide, Ai does not keep his last promise to Estraven, that the star ship will not land in Karhide unless the king clears Estraven's name. "Even I betrayed him," admits Ai, adding a rational explanation that he could not insist on this condition and disregard what Estraven had sacrificed his life for. Does a logical explanation, even if a sound one, mitigate the severity of the betrayal?

MULTIPLICITY OF ANSWERS

The extent of Ai's education in Gethen is manifested in his conversation with the king. Quite boldly Ai makes it clear that both he and Estraven have served the same master, meaning that the motif for their action has been one: to serve humanity. However, while saying it, Ai realizes that this may not be the truth, or at least not the only truth; that it will be just as true to say that Estraven acted out of love for and fidelity to Ai. But this, too, is not completely true, because Estraven loved Ai not less because he identified him with his dead brother Arek. The truth is always complex, presenting us with no clear or certain answers. Once again Ai, and the readers, learn that the Foretellers were right, and the only certain thing is uncertainty.

THE KEYSTONE METAPHOR

The story comes full circle: the setting of the keystone in the arch in the first chapter comes to full fruition in the last chapter. Ai realizes that with Estraven dead, he has to accomplish what Estraven has died for, to set the keystone in the arch. But if in the first chapter the King set an actual keystone in a real arch, in this chapter Ai uses it as a **metaphor** for his entire mission: the creation of a bridge between the planets. Now it can be completed, with Estraven's blood serving as the mystical bonding, just as Estraven told him in the first chapter, "Without the bloodbond the arch would fall." For the mission, at least, a happy ending: a strong and lasting bond between Gethen and the League of the Planets.

THE MEETING OF TWO WORLDS

When the star ship lands safely and Ai, profoundly changed by his experiences in Gethen and his relationship with Estraven, meets his companions from Earth, people divided into men and women, he sees them as freaks of nature, aliens. He is reminded by these Earth companions of his own divided and perpetual sexuality, and he feels disgusted and is literally taken ill.

It has taken Ai more than two years and many profound experiences to accept and love Estraven. Now Ai, lacking Estraven's "grandeur of spirit," has no tolerance for his own people, who have become the Other and the aliens in his eyes. Only when his Gethenian physician visits him and Ai sees "not a man's face and not a woman's, a human face," does he feel some relief.

Ai's success in fulfilling his mission has a tragic price: the pain for the loss of his friend, and the realization that the sexual unity of the Gethenians, their human face, is more advanced and humane than the division into men and women of his own race.

LOVE AND SORROW

Unable to share in the joy of the people of Karhide and of his companions from the star ship, Ai takes a trip to Estraven's home land, from which Estraven had been exiled twenty years earlier. The place is bleak but from his bedroom window Ai can see the forest that lies between the estates of Estre and Stok, of whose war and peace, love and betrayal and final reconciliation, we have learned in the myths of "Estraven the Traitor" (Chapter 9).

A FOOL'S ERRAND

Ai meets Estraven's father and son, but fails to find in either what he longs for: something to remind him of Estraven. Looking for comfort, he finds none. Ai feels that his is a fool's errand, which also gives the title to this final chapter.

Does Le Guin, through Ai, hint that even Ai's mission, his errand to Gethen, is a fool's errand? Ai, who volunteered for the job, seeking to establish alliance between the planets, finds himself in the depth of sorrow, being unable to find solace and peace for himself.

But Ai is mistaken. He fails to see that solace is waiting for him in Estraven's son, Sorve, who with the curiosity of a young man wants Ai to tell him how they crossed the Gobrin Ice, how Estraven died, and not least, about other worlds. We can hope that in the telling Ai will be able to experience once again his love for Estraven and find solace.

ENDING: COEXISTENCE OF OPPOSITES

It is characteristic of Le Guin that the ending is a mixed bag of despair, sorrow, and loss as well as of success, achievement, and hope for a harmonious and peaceful future. The sorrow is on the personal level, the hope is on a more general and ephemeral one. Is Le Guin's message that universal peace can be established only at the price of personal loss and sorrow and human blood? Possibly the answer, as for many other questions, is unknown. It is Estraven's youthful son, very much his parent's child, who utters the last words of hope, and with curiosity and enthusiasm wishes to know "other worlds ... other kinds of men, other lives."

GETHENIAN CALENDAR AND CLOCK

In her book, Le Guin introduces a different attitude to time than the one we employ in the West. Modeled on Taoism, her time, like water, though flowing, is always there. On Gethen it is always the Year One. And since we are always in Year One, there is no progress as such, no pushing ahead aggressively, no hurrying. Past and future are counted backwards or forwards from the unitary Now. Time is balanced. A model for this balance of time can be found in the Chinese civilization. Le Guin admits that when she wrote her book, she did not know that the Chinese calendar has no linear counting system, such as ours that dates from birth of Christ. Le Guin is ingenious in her invention of an entire calendar system, although most readers will get lost in the multitude of new and unfamiliar words.

THE LEFT HAND OF DARKNESS

CRITICS RESPOND TO THE LEFT HAND OF DARKNESS

Publication of *The Left Hand of Darkness* in 1969 was at first more shrouded in darkness than flooded in light, at least by the mainstream publications. *Publishers Weekly* (Jan 27, 1969), an influential professional publication that heralds the arrival of new books, was far from enthusiastic. The anonymous critic found the book to be "difficult reading with an over-abundance of invented language and unpronounceable names, and endless rosters of conspirators." The critic admits that the journey on the ice is "exciting" but "the rest of the book is confusing unless you are very up on intergalactic politics."

The fact that this critic sarcastically called the new planet Gethen "retarded" only suggests that he misread the book, and that the message of the book-a "thought-experiment" in love and betrayal, equality of the sexes, or the coexistence of opposites-was lost on him.

Other mainstream American publications ignored the book altogether, even when it won the prestigious Hugo and Nebula Awards for best science fiction novel of 1969. Their editors did not consider science fiction novels to be serious literature. The prevalent criticism was, and still is, that in science fiction novels, ideas take precedence over language, the content over form, the "what" over the "how." Even Le Guin herself said (*Publishers Weekly*, June 14, 1976) that science fiction is "full of trash presently ... but the trash is lessening." Consequently, as Darko Suvin, a Yugoslavian-born Canadian critic, wrote (*College English*, Dec. 1972), science fiction had been pushed into "a reservation or ghetto."

The lack of serious criticism of *The Left Hand of Darkness*, as well as of science fiction novels in general, irks Le Guin. In her essay, "A Citizen of Mondath" (1973), she laments that, because there was so little literary criticism of science fiction, "the writer is almost his only critic." In spite of having dedicated readers, science fiction had been, and largely still is, considered a marginal **genre** in the academic world.

Even across the Atlantic, where both the press and the public tend to take works of the imagination more seriously, the literary press was lukewarm. The critic of the prestigious *Times Literary Supplement of London* (January 8, 1970), in a survey of several science fiction books, commented that the beginning of Le Guin's book "would kill any novel, full of strange names, numbers, and hesitations." This critic, too, did not delve deeply into the meaning of the book, and after giving us a short synopsis of the plot, regretted, good-humoredly, that Le Guin hesitates to "treat us to a good dose of kemmer" and "sticks to her topography."

But within the science fiction milieu, *The Left Hand of Darkness* became an immediate success, hailed as Le Guin's best work so far. Not only did it win the most important awards in the field, but it attracted the notice of a number of scholars.

Brian W. Aldiss, in his history of science fiction, *Billion Year Spree* (1973), writes that "Le Guin is a rarity in that she writes beautifully. Not prettily. Beautifully. Her prose is a pleasure to read."

Douglas Barbour, a Canadian critic, was the first to study several of Le Guin's novels (*Science Fiction Studies*, Spring 1974). He detected common **themes** and images running parallel in her books and concluded that "the whole of *The Left Hand of Darkness* is a masterful example of form creating content."

Suvin, considered by many to be the best science fiction critic today, said that *The Left Hand of Darkness* is the "extremely realistic psychological, sociological, even political insight" of two people who overcome their alienation to achieve intimacy and understanding.

In 1975, the scholarly publication *Science Fiction Studies* dedicated its entire November issue to a serious study of Le Guin's writing, declaring her to be "a leading American Science Fiction Writer," whose work "is marked by an artistic originality."

Martin Bickman's essay, "Le Guin's *The Left Hand of Darkness*: Form and Content" (*Science Fiction Studies*, March 1977) suggests ways to reconcile form and content in the novel in a "functional, organic, and aesthetically meaningful way." Bickman views Ai as the "structuring consciousness" of the narrative: he tells his story and also selects and arranges the myths and legends and excerpts from Estraven's diary. The order he imposes suggests the understanding and insight he has gained on Gethen.

In the series *Popular Writers of Today* (1976), George Edgar Slusser claims that Le Guin's writing has been good from the start and that she is "one of the best writers currently working" in the field. Slusser was the first to make a comprehensive study of Le Guin's novels, dealing with thematic and moral elements. He argues that Taoism is "the strongest single force" in all her writing.

However, her legitimization as an important contemporary fiction writer, and not narrowly as SF novelist, was made by the literary critic Robert Scholes, in his book *Structural Fabulation* (1975). Scholes maintains that with the *Left Hand of Darkness,* Le Guin displays "powers so remarkable that only full and serious critical scrutiny can begin to reveal her value as a writer." Her gift is to merge fantasy and **realism** and to "naturalize the supernatural." The book, he writes, is rich and very moving and better written than most science fiction writing. The power of the book lies in the way "it interweaves all its levels and combines all its voices and values into an ordered, balanced whole." If he had to choose one writer whose work is "of compelling power and beauty, employing a language that is fully adequate to this aesthetic intention, that writer would be the Good Witch of the West," Ursula K. Le Guin.

Joan Jotte Hall (*The New Republic,* February 7, 1976) remarks that Le Guin, like the novelist Doris Lessing, "has crossed ...the traditional line between fiction and science-fiction. Ursula Le Guin is capable of a healthy blurring of genres."

While within the domain of science fiction literature and criticism, long and serious articles analyze Le Guin's novels and stories from every possible point of view, only slowly and hesitantly does her reputation make its way to the mainstream of fiction criticism.

John Updike, in *The New Yorker* (June 23, 1980), under the title "Imagining Things," dedicates two full pages to Le Guin. He accredits her writing with "mainstream tact, color, and intelligence." Like Ray Bradbury and Kurt Vonnegut, she has recently "entered what is hailed as 'mainstream fiction'." He calls *The Left Hand of Darkness* "a heartwarming tale of emerging statehood and evolved androgyny on a wintry planet." He claims that her fantasies carry more "earthy substance" and are more relevant to our present life on Earth than the usual science fiction books. He refers to an illuminating quote by Peter Beagle (in his introduction to *The Lord of the Rings*): "the Sixties were the time when the word progress lost its ancient holiness, and escape stopped being comically obscene." Fantasies offer "a green alternative to each day's madness here in a poisoned world."

However, harsh criticism came from an unexpected source. The distinguished Polish science fiction writer, Stanislaw Lem, wrote in *Science Fiction Commentary* (November 1971) that in *The Left Hand of Darkness*, Le Guin "would not create, could not create, or did not know how to create the cruel harshness of the individual's destiny" in a system in which ambisexual individuals, in their kemmer, or sexual period, become, without knowing beforehand, either male or female. The fact that Winter's people do not know what sex they will assume in their next cycle, whether they are going to "impregnate or get impregnated" must put them under great psychological stress. What if someone who becomes male loves someone who becomes female, then in a later cycle both become male or female: do they simply go to seek different partners? What about love relationships, long-term affection? They must experience much grief. To Lem, this state of affairs seems "hellish."

Although Lem agrees that the novel is very well written, and the alien civilization contains "richness and variety," it is not consistent. Whatever Le Guin's intentions, "she has written about a planet where there are no women, but only men ... garments, manners of speech, mores, and behavior, are masculine ... the male element has remained victorious over the female one."

In a later issue of the same publication (April 1972), Le Guin seems to be very defensive. She first clarifies that when two Gethenians are in kemmer, the second of the pair will always develop into the sex opposite to the first. Then she asks whether anyone can show her a passage or a dialogue in which Estraven or any Gethenian, "does or says something that only a man could or would do or say." We feel this way, she claims, because we are not used to imagining women "as scheming prime ministers, haulers of sledges," etc. She admits, however, that the use of the masculine pronoun influences the reader's imagination.

Joanna Russ, a feminist critic and science fiction writer (*The Female Man*, 1987), supported Lem's criticism. She wrote (*Magazine of Fantasy and Science Fiction*, March 1975) that in Le Guin's novel the ambisexual theme failed because the people on Gethen seem to be exclusively male. Moreover, she argued that "the family structure is not fully explained," and that "child-rearing is left completely in the dark." As for the writing itself, she said that it is too much telling and not enough showing.

Four years later (1976), in her essay "Is Gender Necessary?", Le Guin admits that one of the book's flaws is that it lacks detailed descriptions of a Gethenian's home life. We are told about the Gethenians' sexual cycle, but we are not shown it. We are told that Estraven is also a woman, but we are given little opportunity to see, feel or sense him as a woman. "I left out too much," she agrees. "One does not see Estraven as a mother, with his children, in any role which we automatically perceive as 'female'. ... This is a real flaw of the book."

Still, eleven years later (1987), in a revision of this same essay now called "Is Gender Necessary? Redux," Le Guin becomes her own most severe critic. About her former defensiveness, she comments, "This is bluster. I had opened a can of worms and was trying hard to shut it." Some of the revisions she makes are especially revealing: he, the male pronoun that excludes women, is changed into the inclusive they. "If I had realized how the pronouns I used shaped, directed, controlled my own thinking, I might have been 'cleverer'." In addition she criticizes the fact that she refrained from exploring homosexuality in *The Left Hand of Darkness.*

Since the publication of *The Left Hand of Darkness*, five books wholly dedicated to the scholarly study of Le Guin's writing have appeared, in addition to essays in numerous collections on science fiction writing.

In *New Worlds for Old* (1974), David Ketterer offers an interesting critical commentary on *The Left Hand of Darkness.* He maintains that the action of the novel is often arbitrary, and that the plot is possible without any mention of the Gethenians' ambisexuality or of Gethen's cold climate, both of which are controlled more by Le Guin's philosophy but are not integrated in the plot. The essential weakness of the novel, he says, is "making sense" of it because it is Le Guin's beliefs that "almost mechanically... determine the various turns of the plot." Although he agrees that the novel is "skillfully integrated" and "woven," he reiterates that "the plot is unfortunately subordinate to the overly conscious use of mythic material."

Joe De Bolt, in his book *Ursula Le Guin: Voyager to Inner Lands and to Outer Space* (1979), claims that as "the walls enclosing the science fiction ghetto were crumbling both from within and without, Le Guin's fiction began to be read alongside mainstream literature."

In her book *Ursula K. Le Guin* (1984), Charlotte Spivack notes that Le Guin's reputation as an "outstanding writer" is growing constantly. Le Guin, who at sixty is at the peak of her career, may still surprise her readers: her recent books show that she is still experimenting with new forms. "Whether she will, as some have speculated, turn to mainstream fiction or whether she will, as others have predicted, create yet new and richer forms of fantasy, remains to be seen."

GLOSSARY OF LE GUIN'S INVENTED WORDS

Dothe

A short period of supreme energy and strength, entered by the Gethenians at will.

Ekumen League of the Planets

3000 nations on 83 planets. The Ekumen's purpose is to develop communication, trade, and harmony between planets.

Erhenrang

The capital of Karhide, one of the two states on the planet of Gethen.

Fastness

A religious retreat of the Handdara cult, and its only fixed locale. People can stay there a day or a lifetime.

Foretellers

Masters of prediction in the Handdara Cult.

Gethen

A distant planet where the story's action takes place. It is also called Winter, because of its bitterly cold climate.

Handdara

The mythical cult or religion of the state of Karhide (modeled by the author on Chinese Taoism). One of its principles is the coexistence of opposites.

Hemmens

The most prevalent tree on Winter, a conifer with thick, pale scarlet needles.

Ignorance

In the Handdara sense: a positive state of mind. It means ignoring the abstraction and holding fast to the thing itself.

Karhide

An anarchic state on Gethen, governed by King Argaven.

Kemmer

A short, cyclical period of sexual activity (estrus).

Kemmerhouse

A place in every community open to everyone, where people in "kemmer" - sexual heat - can find available partners.

Kemmering Group

A group of people who regularly meet in their "kemmer" phase.

Kemmering Vow

Bonding for life, a personal commitment between two people.

Mishnory

The capital of Orgoreyn, one of the two states on Gethen.

Nusuth No matter

It really means inactivity or noninterference, and serves as a typical Handdara response to many situations.

Orgoreyn

A totalitarian state on Gethen.

Shifgrethor

Pride relationships between individuals. It is the ability to maintain harmony in any relationship and dictates the way Gethenians relate to each other.

War

Le Guin's own definition: "Mass Rape, when an army (male, of course) invades."

Untrance The Handdara discipline of Presence

A kind of trance involving self-loss through extreme sensual awareness.

Year One

The current year in the Gethenian calendar.

Yomesh

The official religion of Orgoreyn. Its followers prefer light and condemn darkness.

THE LEFT HAND OF DARKNESS

IDEAS FOR PAPERS, ORAL REPORTS, AND CLASS DISCUSSION

1. Simone de Beauvoir's *The Second Sex* (France 1949, United States 1953), is considered the bible of the feminists. Read de Beauvoir's introduction to her book and compare her ideas to those of Le Guin's in *The Left Hand of Darkness*. Pay special attention to the idea of the Other. In what ways is Le Guin's ambisexual society the answer to Simone de Beauvoir's harsh criticism of the inequality between the sexes?

2. Le Guin has said that the question "What is a woman?" provoked her to write *The Left Hand of Darkness*. In what way does or does not the book answer this question? What are the arguments that the book suggests for a possible answer to the question: What are the differences between men and women?

3. A year before publication of *The Left Hand of Darkness*, Le Guin wrote a short story, "Winter's King," directly related to the novel. Sometime after the publication of the novel, she revised her short story in a meaningful way.

a. Compare the two versions of "Winter's King." How do the changes Le Guin has made influence the content, the characters, and the reader?

b. Write a detailed essay in which you compare Le Guin's two versions of "Winter's King" with her novel.

4. Discuss the ambisexual society, the most original invention of Le Guin's *The Left Hand of Darkness*. In what ways does this invention serve the overall idea of Le Guin's book?

5. Choose two scenes which feature Ai and Estraven (maybe the first time they are alone together in the first chapter, and when they are fugitives on the Gobrin Ice) and rewrite them so that the male pronoun relating to Estraven will be female. How will the feminine pronoun affect Estraven's character, the relationship between the two, the mood, and the general impact of the narrative?

6. Chapter 7, "The Question of Sex," was written by a woman Investigator, which allows us an inkling of the way a woman looks at the Gethenians. Now, what if the Envoy had been a woman? How would the Gethenians have appeared to her? Would her own exclusively female identity have seemed a weakness, compared to their ambisexuality, as Ai's maleness does? Would she identify with their female side and find their "maleness" an intrusion?

7. Good writing happens when ideas and form coalesce to a point where you don't know when one ends and the other begins. Discuss the relationships between Le Guin's ideas and intentions and the story she has written.

8. In his book *New Worlds for Old*, the Canadian critic David Ketterer claims that Le Guin's philosophy dictates the plot of her book; the plot can be summarized, and could well exist, without either the Gethenian ambisexuality, or the cold climate on Winter. Write an essay on one of these points, supporting or refuting Ketterer's claim. Support your thesis with examples.

9. In complete opposition to Ketterer, the Canadian critic Douglas Barbour argues that "the whole [of *The Left Hand of Darkness*] is a masterful example of form creating content." Analyze *The Left Hand of Darkness* from Barbour's point of view and bring examples to support your opinion.

10. Joanna Russ, a critic and a science fiction writer herself, argues that *The Left Hand of Darkness* is too much telling and not enough showing. Discuss her argument, and cite examples to support or refute it.

11. Compare Theodore Sturgeon's androgynous society of the Ledom in *Venus Plus X* (1960) and that of the Gethenians in Le Guin's *The Left Hand of Darkness*.

12. The British critic George Steiner stated that "language is the main instrument of man's refusal to accept the world as it is." Discuss this statement in relation to *The Left Hand of Darkness*.

13. Do you consider the society of Karhide on Gethen to be a utopian society? Look up one or more definitions of utopia and discuss them in view of the novel.

14. Read Joanna Russ's novel *The Female Male* and compare it - theme, plot, handling of ideas, use of language-with *The Left Hand of Darkness.*

15. Critic George Slusser argues that Taoism is "the strongest single force" underlying all of Le Guin's novels. Read Alan Watts' *Tao: The Watercourse Way,* and/or Chang Chungyuan's *Creativity and Taoism* (or any other book on Taoism you prefer), and discuss *The Left Hand of Darkness* as a reflection of Taoist philosophy.

16. In her introduction to *The Left Hand of Darkness,* Le Guin maintains that science fiction is not about the future but about the present. Critics have mentioned that both Karhide and Orgoreyn are meant as criticism of present societies. In what ways is her novel critical of our contemporary society?

17. In her introduction to her book, Le Guin says that when we read a good novel, we may find "that we're a bit different from what we were before we read it, that we have been changed a little." Think about some novels you have read that influenced you to change, even if just a little. What must a novel have in order to be able to change you? Is *The Left Hand of Darkness* in this category? Explain your answer.

18. Read one other novel by Le Guin, possibly *The Dispossessed.* Compare it to *The Left Hand of Darkness.* Discuss and compare Le Guin's themes, techniques, and structures in each novel.

19. Some critics argue that the real **theme** of the book is communication. Discuss the different levels of

communication dealt with in the novel. What is Le Guin's overall message about communication?

20. In her essay "The Child and the Shadow" (*The Language of the Night*), Le Guin recounts a fascinating fairy tale by Hans Christian Andersen, in order to explain her idea of the shadow. Discuss the idea of the shadow in the fairy tale and in *The Left Hand of Darkness.*

21. Many critics claim that Le Guin's journey to outer space is in fact an inner journey into the unconscious. Discuss this double journey in view of the novel. How does Le Guin achieve this double journey?

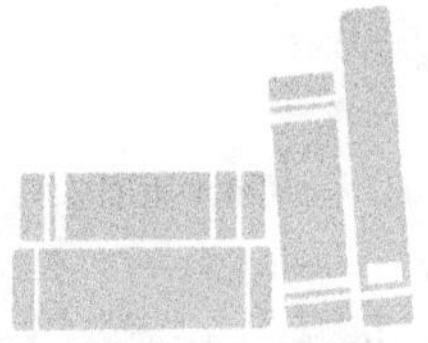

SELECTED BIBLIOGRAPHY

PRIMARY SOURCES: WRITINGS BY URSULA LE GUIN

Novels

Rocannon's World. New York: Ace Books, 1966.

Planet of Exile. New York: Ace Books, 1966.

City of Illusions. New York: Ace Books, 1967.

A Wizard of Earthsea. Berkeley: Parnassus Press, 1968.

The Left Hand of Darkness. New York: Ace Books, 1969.

The Tomb of Atuan. New York: Atheneum, 1971.

The Lathe of Heaven. New York; Charles Scribner's Sons, 1971.

The Farthest Shore. New York: Atheneum, 1972.

The Dispossessed. New York: Harper & Row, 1974.

The Word for World Is Forest. New York: 1976.

Very Far Away from Anywhere Else. New York: Atheneum, 1976.

The Eye of the Heron. In *Millennial Women*, Virginia Kidd, ed., New York: Delacorte Press, 1978; New York: Harper & Row, 1983.

Malafrena. New York: Berkley-Putnam, 1979.

The Beginning Place. New York: Harper & Row, 1980.

Always Coming Home. New York: Harper & Row, 1985.

Short Story Collections

The Wind's Twelve Quarters. New York: Harper & Row, 1975.

Orsinian Tales. New York: Harper & Row, 1976; New York: Bantam, 1977.

The Compass Rose. New York: Harper & Row, 1982.

Poetry Collections

Wild Angels. Santa Barbara: Capra Press, 1975.

Hard Words. New York: Harper & Row, 1981.

Essay Collections

From Elfland to Poughkeepsie. Portland: Pendragon Press, 1973.

Dreams Must Explain Themselves. New York: Algol Press, 1975.

The Language of the Night. New York, G.P. Putnam's Sons, 1979.

Dancing at the Edge of the World. New York, Grove Press, 1989.

Children's Stories

Solomon Leviathan's 931st Trip Around the World. Middlesex, Eng.: Puffin, 1976.

Leese Webster. New York: Atheneum, 1979.

WORKS EDITED BY LE GUIN

Nebula Award Stories Eleven. New York: Harper & Row, 1977.

Interfaces. (With Virginia Kidd) New York: Ace Books, 1980.

SECONDARY SOURCES FOR RESEARCH ON LE GUIN

Works Wholly About Le Guin

Bucknail, Barbara J. *Ursula Le Guin.* New York: Ungar Publishing Co., 1981.

De Bolt, Joe, ed. *Ursula Le Guin: Voyager to Inner Lands and to Outer Space.* Port Washington, N.Y.: Kennikat Press, 1979.

Olander, Joseph D. and Martin Greenberg, eds. *Ursula K. Le Guin.* New York: Taplinger Publishing Co., Inc., 1979.

Slusser, George Edgar. *The Farthest Shores of Ursula K. Le Guin*. San Bernardino, California: Borgo Press, 1976.

Spivak, Charlotte. *Ursula Le Guin*. Boston: Twayne Publishers, 1984.

Works Partly About Le Guin

Authors in the News. Volume I, Gale, 1976.

Anna, Pamela J. "New Worlds, New Words: Androgyny in Feminist Science Fiction," *Science Fiction Studies* 5,2 (July 1978): 143–56.

Aldiss, Brian W. *Billion Year Spree: The True History of Science Fiction*. Garden City, N.Y.: Doubleday, 1973.

Barron, Neil. *Anatomy of Wonder: Science Fiction*. New York and London: R. R. Bowker Company, 1976.

Bickman, Martin. "Le Guin's *The Left Hand of Darkness*: Form and Content," *Science Fiction Studies* 4, 1 (March 1977): 42–47.

Bretnor, Reginald, ed. *Science Fiction, Today and Tomorrow*. New York: Harper & Row, 1974.

Cogell, Elizabeth Cummins. "Setting as Analogue to Characterization in Ursula Le Guin." *Extrapolation* 18, no. 2 (1977): 131–41.

Clareson, Thomas D. *Voices for the Future*. Bowling Green, Ohio: Bowling Green University Popular Press, 1976.

Galbreath, Robert. "Holism, Openness and the Other: Le Guin's Use of the Occult." *Science Fiction Studies* 7, 1 (March 1980): 36–48.

Dictionary of Literary Biography. Volume VIII, Part I: Twentieth-Century American Science Fiction Writers. Gale, 1981.

Jameson, Frederic. "World-Reduction in Le Guin: The Emergence of Utopian Narrative." *Science Fiction Studies* 2 (Nov. 1975): 221–30.

Ketterer, David. *New Worlds for Old: The Apocalyptic Imagination*. Bloomington: Indiana University Press, 1974.

Nicholls, Peter, ed. *The Science Fiction Encyclopedia*. Garden City, N.Y.: Doubleday, 1979.

Nudelman, Rafail. "An Approach to the Structure of Le Guin's SF." *Science Fiction Studies* 2,3 (Nov. 1975): 210–20.

Sargent, Pamela, ed. *Women of Wonder*. New York: Random House, 1975.

Scholes, Robert, *Structural Fabulation*. Notre Dame, Indiana: University of Notre Dame Press, 1975.

_______, "Science Fiction as Conscience: John Brunner and Ursula K. Le Guin," *New Republic 175* (October 30, 1976): 39.

Suvin, Darko. "Parables of De-Alienation: Le Guin's Widdershins Dance." *Science Fiction Studies* 2, 3 (Nov. 1975): 265–74.

Walker, Jeanne Murray. "Myths, Exchange, and History in *The Left Hand of Darkness*." *Science Fiction Studies* 6 (July 1979): 180–89.

Wood, Susan. "Discovering Worlds: The Fiction of Ursula Le Guin." *Voices of the Future*, Vol. 2. Bowling Green, Ohio: Bowling Green University Popular Press, 1978.

www.ingramcontent.com/pod-product-compliance
Lightning Source LLC
Chambersburg PA
CBHW061518050726
47593CB00002B/632
9781645425205